saving sammy

saving sammy

Curing the Boy
Who Caught OCD

Beth Alison Maloney

CROWN PUBLISHERS
New York

All rights reserved.
Published in the United States by Crown Publishers,
an imprint of the Crown Publishing Group,
a division of Random House, Inc., New York.
www.crownpublishing.com

CROWN and the Crown colophon are registered
trademarks of Random House, Inc.

Library of Congress Cataloging-in-Publication Data is available
upon request.

ISBN 978-0-307-46183-4

Printed in the United States of America

Design by Cindy LaBreacht

10 9 8 7 6 5 4 3 2 1

First Edition

This book is dedicated to three courageous doctors
who have changed the face of medicine:

Drs. Barry J. Marshall and J. Robin Warren,
who proved that stomach ulcers are caused by bacterial infections.

Dr. Susan E. Swedo at the National Institute of Mental Health
for her pioneering research about the infectious cause
of obsessive-compulsive disorder.

CONTENTS

[vii]

CONTENTS

What if the
mightiest word
is love?

———————————————

Elizabeth Alexander

saving
sammy

Dear Dr. Geller

Daniel A. Geller, M.D.
Director, Pediatric OCD Program
Massachusetts General Hospital
Child and Adolescent Psychiatry, Yawkey 6A
55 Fruit Street
Boston, MA 02114

Dear Dr. Geller:

Enclosed please find the completed registration forms for my son Sammy. As you know, we are coming to see you next week on the advice of Dr. Catherine Nicolaides of Marlton, New Jersey.

I thought it would be helpful to provide you with this overview of Sammy's history and current behaviors. The problems suddenly started sixteen months ago, shortly after he turned twelve. Among other things, he stopped eating and lost twenty pounds.

Sammy does not seem to have obsessions, but he certainly has compulsions. His compulsions fall into two categories: rituals and avoidance.

He likes to start the morning with something he calls "the usual." When he asks for the usual, that means he wants five drinks: milk, orange juice, apple juice, pink lemonade, and grape juice. He pinches his nose when he sips and drinks them in a certain order. The drinks do not all have to be at the same level in the cups. They do not have to be in any particular cups. He just needs all five juices, every morning.

He has to go through a series of complicated motions before he'll go into the bathroom, before he comes back into the house from being outside, when he first gets into the house, or when he walks through a parking lot—in short, everywhere he goes. This might involve swirling his legs, ducking, crawling, rolling his head on his neck, stepping sideways, or high-stepping over a nonexistent barrier. At our home, he has to do these in the exact same spot each time. The ritual itself might be different, but the spot does not vary. It is a major effort for him to walk upstairs in the house. He has to hold his breath while he runs up the stairs, stopping midway on the landing to duck his head into a cabinet and gasp for air. When he needs to do a whole series of compulsive behaviors, we have to leave the room. I don't know if this is so that we don't see him or so he can give the routine his full attention—and thus do it exactly right.

There are many things he avoids, including all mats, doors, and faucets. He does not shower or brush his teeth except at the hotel where we stay in New Jersey (when we go to see Dr. Nicolaides). Even then, he does not use soap. He told me that he is going to try to take showers at home, at noon, on Saturdays, beginning this weekend.

He is very careful about what he touches and what touches him. Hugs are out of the question. He does not flush the toilet. He does not wash his hands. He does not touch light switches. He does not touch his food. He uses either utensils (only those with a silver handle) or a paper towel or napkin to hold, for example, a slice of toast. He will not open a door (house or car). He will not step on a rug. He avoids or jumps over the white stripes in a parking lot.

He has started answering the telephone, using a tissue to grasp the receiver, but he holds it away from his ear and shouts. At the computer, he previously covered the mouse with a napkin, but lately he touches it directly. He prefers to run outside to urinate, rather than enter the bathroom (about which he thinks I don't know). But because he cannot touch a door handle, he must find someone to open the outside door. If he can't find someone, he will use the bathroom because I make certain the door is always left ajar.

He will not wear a coat or jacket. If it's raining, he gets wet. If it's freezing, he gets cold.

Last year he would not wear socks or shoes. Now he wears socks all the time, wears shoes whenever he goes outside, and cringes if anyone is in bare feet. Consequently, we must all wear socks at all times. Even sandals are a problem. The issue is primarily bare toes, but heels are also troublesome.

He only likes to wear certain colors—preferably khaki and green. For a while he wore the same clothes for months, but thankfully he now changes them at least once a week.

He would never hurt himself or anyone else.

If he thinks he is being too demanding, he gets teary-eyed.

He used to ask me to do certain rituals (such as carry his food a certain way), but I wasn't especially cooperative. He no longer asks.

I'm tired just from typing all this loopy stuff, so it must be a full day's work for him to keep it straight.

He is not able to attend school. A tutor comes to the house. He stands and moves in the shape of an upside-down L.

Prior to the onset sixteen months ago, Sammy did not exhibit any of the behaviors outlined above, with one exception. Four years ago, in the winter of third grade, he started having a tough time. He would curl the fingers of his left hand up and into his sleeve. We eventually figured out that he had a learning disability in reading. With a special reading program in place to address this challenge, the hand gradually dropped down and out of the sleeve.

I have enclosed a chart tracking Sammy's medication history.

Thank you very much, and we look forward to meeting you.

Odds are he'll be the one wearing the khaki pants and green shirt.

Beth Maloney
Kennebunkport, Maine

cc: Dr. Catherine Nicolaides
Dr. Conner Moore

sixteen
months
earlier

1

Eyes Shut Tight

I was on my way from the house to our van, struggling under the weight of another full moving box, when I caught sight of Sammy in the side yard. My just-turned-twelve-year-old's eyes were scrunched up tight, sealing out the daylight. His hands were extended in front of him, and he was feeling his way around as if he were blind. Catching a breath, I rested my box on a granite boulder and watched.

Summer was in full swing in Maine. The sunlight bouncing off his hair had probably bounced off a wave just moments before. When we lived in California, his hair would have been singed platinum by this time of year. In Kennebunkport, the sun was gentler, so his hair was golden brown.

Just two weeks before, Sammy had ended his fifth grade year with a pocketful of math awards. All his hard work to overcome a learning disability in reading had paid off, too. He was one of the finalists in a civic oration contest. I'd sat in the

grade school gym, on a blue folding chair, and been surprised
to hear him speak. In front of the audience, he was charis-
matic.

He puzzled me lately, though. In the last few days, I'd seen
him walking around the house with his eyes shut.

"In addition to everything else, I've got a little blind boy,"
I'd told my mother when she called to see how things were
lining up for the move.

He also began using his hands to navigate. He touched his
way around everything, inside and out: interior walls, exterior
sidings, the swing set, the stone wall, even feeling his way into
the bathroom. I'd shrugged it off. Kids do weird things sometimes. I knew that; I'd watched my three boys for years.

This was bugging me, though, so I sucked in a deep breath
of salt air and called over to him.

"Sammy, what are you doing?"

He didn't answer at first, but that was not unusual for him.
He was often deeply lost in his own sweet world. What passed
for daydreaming was always something more. At home, he
combed the beaches. At school, he walked the fields. He'd
readily join in if the other children asked, but—if not—he was
content to walk alone and ponder.

I cupped my hands around my mouth and shouted over in
my best cheerleader voice: "Hey! Sammy! What are you doing?
Why are your eyes shut?"

He turned his head toward me, cocking his ear to the side.
His slender face was contorted from the effort of keeping his
eyes pinned shut.

"Memorizing!" he shouted back.

I watched him move toward the lilac bushes. Now it made
sense.

I HATED MOVING, TOO—EVEN though the new house was
just a few miles away. I would miss everything about this place:
the wild sea roses, the tall cattails, the rippled basin of the
cove that remained when the water retreated at low tide, the
island that was just a short walk away. This spot I had rented,
the one we were leaving, had saved us. The sparkling sea, the
baby lobsters in tide pools, the seaweed waving from the rolling
tide: they had all nurtured us.

My first thought had been for my sons—not for me—
when I learned that my marriage was over. I was determined
that they be whole. My broken heart, held together with
bands of love for my boys, led us to this place. Here we had
healed and become a new unit.

For years, I had viewed an endless stream of houses with
For Sale signs propped up in the front yard. My criteria were
specific: always in Kennebunkport and not more than a five-
mile radius from our beloved cove. Real estate agents grew
tired of me. Still, I persisted. Sometimes I would take the kids.
They would propel themselves from floor to floor, then be
back in the front hall before I had seen a second room.

"Can we go now?" they'd ask as a chorus, their three small
faces shining up at me while they hopped impatiently from foot
to foot.

In the end, the new house had been there all along. It
waited for us in the woods by a marsh and—poof—materialized
within days after the court issued the divorce papers. This

time the kids had smiled up at me and nodded yes to this home.

I was concerned about moving Sammy. He was the one most attached to the sea. He endlessly walked the neighborhood, prowled the cove, poked for crabs, and climbed the chunks of ledge that jutted along the coast. He brought me flowers and sea lavender from his journeys. I called him my wanderer. Once, when he was eight, he went for a walk down to the water and vanished. After an hour of frantic searching, I found him almost half a mile away from the house.

"Sammy!" I shouted when I finally spotted him. He was hopping boulders along the coast. When he heard my voice, he stopped suddenly and faced me, puzzled by my concern.

"I've been searching for an hour!" I was crying by then. Regret took over his face when he realized where he was and how long he had been gone.

"I'm sorry, Mom," he said with teary brown eyes.

I REMEMBERED ALL OF this while I stood and watched him in the yard, his eyes determinedly clamped shut. I remembered the terror that tore through my heart when I thought I might have lost him. Four years later, it still sent a chill down my spine.

I was jolted out of my thoughts when the front door to the house slammed. My youngest, James, plunged out carrying a small box of trinkets. He stopped where I rested and looked up at me with a question in his green eyes. Their sea-glass color matched my own.

"Are you sure, Mom?" he asked for the hundredth time, worried that his friends would not know where we'd moved.

"They'll find us. I promise," I reassured him, patting his blond curls. "Their moms all know where we'll be."

When we first moved here, James was so small he slept in a large empty closet just off my room. He was too grown-up for a crib but not yet ready for a bed, and I wanted him close to me. I put a small mattress on the floor and gated the doorway. He filled the closet space with treasures from the sea.

On steamy days when the tide retreated, we meandered barefoot over to the island. When it was chilly, we pulled on our knee-high rubber boots and sloshed along. We picked a path between the moorings and the boats temporarily docked on the sand. We found shells and seaweed and errant buoys. We watched gulls scoop tiny sparkling fish from small pools of water. There were bits of sea glass on the island, some for our pockets and all for good luck. We found bait bags that had escaped from lobster traps. Into the bags we dropped rocks rubbed smooth by the surf. James was seven now. We still took our walks, but he preferred collecting friends instead.

I turned back toward Sammy. His arms were stretched in front of him, like those of a blind person lost in the woods. He slowly felt his way past the cedar swing set and over to a group of trees. He stopped and ran his fingers through the deeply grooved bark of a fat pine.

I shrugged my shoulders, picked up my box, and started off, with James trailing behind. We dropped our belongings in the van and turned back to the house. James detoured for the swing set. Along the slate walk to the porch, broken bits of concrete crunched under my feet. I had first crunched along that walk when I rented the place, and I'd known from the first crunch that the house would be right for us.

I stepped through the front door and into semidarkness. The wraparound porch had been closed in, cutting the sun from the room. As my eyes adjusted, I spotted Josh, my oldest, bent over a box in the nook that we called the den. He was packing up the computer. Packing anything electronic was Josh's job. When we got to the new place, he planned to build a computer. At fifteen, he was scrawny, with dark eyes and thick hair that bordered between brown and black. None of my boys had inherited the burgundy tones of my auburn hair.

JOSH IS A MATH and science guy. Even when he was little, he found math everywhere. At home, he precisely measured the ingredients we needed to bake scrumptious cakes and cookies. At the grocery store, he mentally calculated which item was best to purchase based on the price per ounce. He was intrigued by strategy, and one of his favorite pastimes became playing chess.

"He joins in the class discussions," his fourth-grade teacher told me, "but quickly takes things to another level."

Josh enjoyed challenging equations, but he found the more basic assignments tiresome. When he was in fifth grade, he burst into my upstairs office one afternoon, waving his language arts workbook.

"Just tell me when you've ever used language arts!" he shouted.

I looked up from the files and legal papers that were piled all over my desk.

"All the time," I said, pointing to every corner of my office, including the filing cabinets, and ending with the document displayed on my computer screen.

He threw up his hands and stormed out.

Josh didn't like to study punctuation and sentence structure, but he was a voracious reader. There was always a book tucked into his pocket. He devoured entire series: *Star Wars, His Dark Materials, The Chronicles of Narnia,* and *The Lord of the Rings.* As fast as I brought them home, he'd finish them. He often read *Time* and *Newsweek* while he nibbled his breakfast and his younger brothers slept. One cold winter morning in seventh grade, he wanted to talk about HIV and AIDS.

"Maybe if you could take the blood out of the body," he said, "and heat it to a high enough temperature, the virus might be killed. Then the blood could go back in the body."

I looked at the clock to make sure it was really only five forty-five and we were having this discussion.

"You're thinking about curing AIDS?" I took a sip of tea, hoping the caffeine would push my brain out of sleep mode.

"There's a good article in *Time.*" He nodded, tapping the magazine with his index finger. "But if my idea would work, don't you think someone else would have thought of it already?"

"Maybe not—medical breakthroughs happen all the time." I looked up at the clock. "Better get ready to go, it's almost time to catch the bus."

He stood and bundled himself into his L. L. Bean jacket.

"One thing for sure," I added. "I'd want you on the research team." I sent him off with a hug and thought how lucky I was that he was mine.

"WILL YOU MISS IT here?" I asked him now, looking around, hands on my hips, taking the whole place in.

"Not really." Always honest, Josh reached for a roll of packing tape. He'd never been a fan of the beach or the house.

Beauty is in the eye of the beholder, and this house was no exception. From the outside it looked a bit like a pumpkin. The second-story windows were the eyes. The string of windows that closed in the wraparound porch formed the nose and the mouth. In a prior life, it had been a barn. Someone had long ago decided that it would make a good house and had moved it to this spot. The conversion took place in piecemeal fashion over some years.

At first, it was a camp. One bedroom downstairs was for the owner; the former hayloft was for everyone else. Eventually the hayloft was divided into four small bedrooms. The renovations had been completed haphazardly, basically done whenever the mood struck the owner. As a result, we could count on water to pour in around the front door during heavy storms. The roof leaked. Rain dripped down the sides of the chimney and through the tiny room I used for my office. In the winter, frigid air rushed in through the windows. Mice sometimes ran free through the living room on cold winter nights, and hornets shared the second story with us in the summer. I ignored all that, though, because from the second floor, I could see the ocean and mark the tides with a glance.

I had given up trying to understand why I was so drawn to the sea. It was easier to surrender, which I did, gradually. First a tide chart from the local market stuck haphazardly onto the old refrigerator. Next a tide clock hung at the base of the stairs, then one for the upstairs, too. I rented a kayak for half a day, and before long I owned one. If the tide was high and the weather manageable, off I would go, thinking about everything else I should be doing but—when back at my desk—always glad I went. When business kept me from the water, I felt empty. When the tides lined up for a morning and an evening paddle, I felt full.

As I watched Josh secure the computer box with plastic tape, I glanced at the tide clock hanging near the stairs: two hours to high tide. I'd be out there, slicing my paddle through the thick, salty water and looking for seals. It would be high tide, and so I would go. Chances are, when I got back and pulled my boat up to the beach, Sammy would be poking around the tide pools. He'd wave as he always did and then go back to searching for crabs. I got a lump in my throat when I thought about how much I would miss that.

"Shall I take it out?" Josh asked, interrupting my thoughts; he was pointing to the tightly sealed box.

"Might as well. The more we move, the better." Movers were expensive, and money was always a concern. The more we moved ourselves, the less I'd have to pay them.

Josh picked up the box and headed out. In a few weeks, he was going to a boarding high school for students who excelled in math and science. Attending the Maine School of Science and Mathematics had been his goal since fifth grade. I stood on the front steps and held the door for him. Sammy, eyes closed, ran his fingers along the crannies of the old fieldstone wall.

THE MOVERS SHOWED UP the next day while the kids were at camp. I had dropped them at the camp bus in the morning. Sammy's eyes were open because there was nothing to memorize there, just the parking lot of the one and only local strip mall. He hopped onto the bus with all the other excited campers who defined summer fun as an opportunity to study astronomy, computer programming, or something equally obtuse on a college campus in Portland. No pine trees or lakeside cabins for this group.

I thought of it as "rocket camp" and often wondered how children could be so different from their mothers. I'd spent my summers riding horses. When I wondered about this aloud to my boys, they insisted that I had a hidden math ability.

"So deeply hidden, it got lost," I said, thinking how grateful I was for computer programs that enabled me to balance my checkbook.

"You're good at the computer," Josh pointed out. "You figure stuff out. Remember how you got the printer to work?"

"That's called downloading a patch," I answered.

"Not everyone knows to do that," he said.

"It's that hidden math ability," Sammy agreed.

"It is, Mom," James chimed in.

The things my three liked to discuss over meals—complicated mathematical formulas, difficult games, computer operating systems—left me feeling lost. A favorite pastime was making up intricate characters for role-playing games such as Dungeons & Dragons. They became so engrossed in conversation with one another that they often forgot to eat. When Josh was five, he had me explain the nuances of mortgage financing to him. When Sammy was ten, the grade school's teacher for the gifted program told me that he had the purest math mind the school had ever seen. James, at seven, was already signed up for the rocket camp's course in computer programming.

After the camp bus pulled away, I made a beeline for the house. The Big Movers truck was in the driveway when I pulled up. I had scheduled the move for when camp was in session. I had a tough time grocery shopping when my kids were around, so even the idea of moving a whole house full of stuff while I tripped over three squabbling boys gave me a headache.

The Big Movers boss had given me an estimate over the telephone months earlier.

"Two days," he'd said.

"Don't you want to send someone to look around?" I'd asked.

"Nope."

I guessed this was how they did it in Maine, but now I knew I was in for trouble. The crew leader walked through the house muttering, "Big job. Big job, really big job." He was tall, over six feet, and had to stoop so he didn't bang his head on some of the door frames.

"This, too?" He pointed or nodded in a particular direction.

"Yup," I answered brightly, "and the swing set." I pointed out the window to the cedar extravaganza in the side yard.

He sucked in a deep breath. Then he continued his perusal, raising an eyebrow as he looked in one room or whistling a "whooooooooo hooooooooo" as he ducked into another.

As we visually took the house apart room by room, I realized he was right. Although the place was small, we lived like pack rats. The few boxes we had moved ourselves did not amount to a dent.

"Three-day job," he said.

"The man on the phone said two days," I protested with every inch of my five-foot-two frame.

"Ah-yuh," he agreed. "He tells everyone that, lets the

owners get upset with me." He lifted his Red Sox cap and ran his hand over his thinning hair.

Money flew out the window as I heard myself agree that this was a three-day job.

By midmorning of the second day, the movers and I had bonded. We were packing and sweating and swearing together, and soon I was smoking, too.

"I don't smoke," I said whenever I bummed another Marlboro, revisiting a habit I had broken long before I'd started law school.

On breaks, we hung out by the truck, swapping stories and shooting the breeze. Hell, it was summertime. I made the first cigarette run after lunch to make up for bumming so many. I may have picked up a six-pack while I was there, but I'm not certain of that. I think I had Patty Hearst syndrome, identifying with my captors.

When the kids came home from camp, I had to duck behind the Big Movers truck to catch a smoke. It got complicated because Sammy was doing his oddball thing of stumbling around the yard with his eyes shut. I thought he might knock into me. Sammy was a walking smoke alarm. When he was little, he'd ask random smokers on the street if they realized they were killing themselves.

"Can't you go memorize somewhere else?" I shouted over from behind the truck, waving the smoke away. The cigarette was tucked tightly behind my back just in case he opened his eyes. Moving was starting to make me incredibly cranky. The Marlboros helped, but I needed more. I called my friend Sharon in California.

"Moving is one of the two most stressful things you can do

in life," she said with patience and knowledge, "even more stressful than getting a divorce."

Sharon had not yet been through her own divorce, and I did not agree with her; but I took another puff, let it out slowly, and kept my thoughts to myself. It was one of those things I had learned at some point after forty. A person does not have to say everything on her mind.

Sharon and I first met through the movie business when I lived in California. She was the casting director, and I did the legal work. Our friendship solidified when Sammy and her son ended up in the same nursery school class. Everything about Sharon sparkled—her soft doe eyes, her light brown hair, and her smile—so she doubled as my beauty adviser. She taught me how to apply makeup correctly (little dots) and to put cream on my face at night even when I felt too tired. Best of all, Sharon liked to kayak when she visited.

"I'm smoking," I confessed, feeling terrible about myself.

"You'll stop when it's over," she reassured me.

By the time we hung up, I felt better.

AFTER THREE FULL DAYS of wondering if the move would ever end, everything was finally in the new house. The movers drove off with the Marlboros, and I never touched one again. Josh hooked up the television at the new house and kept an eye on James. Sammy kept me company while I cleaned our old adorable rental by the sea. I swept the porches, washed the floors, and stacked the Corelle plates and bowls for the last time. We had rented it furnished, so the place now looked like it did when we first moved in. Sammy was stretched out on the couch, watching television.

"It feels like we still live here," he called into the kitchen from his spot on the couch.

"Do you miss it already?" I walked the few steps from the kitchen to the living room, wiping my hands on a dish towel.

"When I'm here, I miss it," he said, "but as soon as I'm there, I don't."

I nodded. Sammy and I shared the same emotional responses to most things in life. He was the most different from me of my children and also the most alike.

I took a last look around the place. Then we turned off the television, flicked off the light, locked the front door, and drove away with our memories.

I did not know that it would be a long time before life felt peaceful again.

2

Into the Woods

For the Fourth of July fireworks, Kennebunkport goes to the beach: moms push strollers, dads lug coolers, little ones skip along. Cars search for spaces well before dusk, and boats embark for the sea.

Guests crowd the patio at the Colony Hotel and drink in the summertime scene. Across the street, down on the beach, kids whirl with sparklers, families share stories, and teenagers meet up with friends. Some climb the jetty that borders the harbor pointing the way to the sea; below them boats pass, in all shapes and sizes, gliding their way to the deep. Off in the distance, a ship full of fireworks patiently waits for its cue. With a bang and a burst, the night sky explodes, and the crowd begins to cheer.

Sammy looked forward to the fireworks every year, but not the year we moved.

THE KIDS AND I slept in the den of our new home that first night, with the moving boxes piled around us. Josh and Sammy each grabbed a couch. James and I spread quilts on the floor. I woke early that first morning surrounded by my loving sons. The sun crept gently through the big windows, pushing its way through a blanket of trees. The first thing I noticed was that the sounds were different. The birds near the marsh did not tweet. They screeched.

My first goal was to get Josh set up in his room. I wanted him to feel moved in before he left for school in a few weeks. After Josh was set up, I searched for my sheets and pillows. I wanted to sleep that night in my own, third-floor room with the treetop view.

The kids slept quietly while I organized. Next task was my office. I had to be able to work on Monday. As a single mother with three children, keeping cash flowing was key.

My office is a large loft on the third floor, adjacent to my bedroom. The location was just right: two stories up from what would be the daily ruckus of the den but close enough to monitor when I needed to intervene. With its arched windows and airy height, this loft was the most beautiful spot I had ever worked in. As I moved the heavy law treatises from boxes to shelves, I remembered other offices I had unpacked—the ones in California with designer furniture and marble lobbies. From their oversized windows on a clear day, I might spot Catalina Island resting in the Pacific while I negotiated a deal. Those offices were dramatic, but they did not offer the peace and beauty of the canopy of treetops that surrounded me now.

I needed that peace and beauty. I accepted cases to work as a guardian *ad litem* on behalf of neglected and abused children in Maine. Part courtroom lawyer and part detective, my job was to put it all together for the courts and recommend a course of action. The children's stories—their drug-addicted families, the abuse they suffered, the untreated mental illness—could take its toll. I tried to stay positive, but sometimes the children were so debilitated, their spirits so broken, that my heart knew it was too late. The children's files went into the filing cabinet on the right.

In the left cabinet, I put the files of my California clients. When I'd lived in Los Angeles, I had worked in private law firms and for movie companies. I still had a fair number of clients who called. I enjoyed having my hand in a deal now and again, but I was relieved that my cross-country jaunts had dwindled. When my plane landed back in Boston from a trip to L.A. and I knew that Maine was just a short drive away, I always sighed with relief. I stayed with Sharon whenever I visited California and I loved seeing her, but Maine kept me centered.

"I can't get spiritual here," I told Sharon on one of my many trips west. We were in her kitchen eating sushi, and I fingered the pieces of sea glass that were tucked in my pocket. We had just hiked a dirt trail that spiraled into a canyon off Mulholland Drive. From that bird's-eye view, the power and magnificence of L.A. had always moved me, but no more. Now it felt flat. It was the North Atlantic I hungered for, its constancy and change: always there, yet never the same—high tide, low tide, a smooth sea or dangerous surf.

Los Angeles was always with me, though. It was where I had grown up professionally. My new house in Maine had a California floor plan. Like the homes that cling to canyons in the Hollywood Hills, the kitchen area was on the second floor.

Sounds of stirring drifted up and drew me away from my thoughts. I dropped the last file into its place and went downstairs to busy myself in the kitchen. One by one, the boys came upstairs as I popped frozen waffles into the toaster. Some days I stumbled over their names as they dashed wildly about me in circles—"James-I-mean-Josh-I-mean-Sammy-no-James!"— but I always knew who was who. On mornings like this, when they were sleepy and slow, I tagged the right name with the right son.

"Who wants to go next?" I asked cheerily while they smeared maple syrup on their toaster waffles. We perched on stools in the bright, sunny kitchen in the house we owned. It felt great!

"Josh is done. Shall I unpack Sammy or James?" I poured grape juice for each of them.

"Do James," answered Sammy. "I'm okay on the couch."

I UNPACKED NONSTOP for the rest of the weekend. When I finished a box, I sliced through the packing tape and folded it flat with a flourish. By Sunday night, the pile had grown respectably. There were still full boxes everywhere, but there was progress. The kitchen was functioning. The boys were in their rooms. I knew where my clothes were. My computer was hooked up, and I would be able to take a few calls. There was one week of rocket camp left, and my schedule was purposefully light. I knew that we would be in good shape by the following weekend. Sammy's bed was ready, but he said he wanted to stay on the couch in the den for a while more. Whatever worked for him was okay with me.

Climbing into bed on Sunday night, completely spent, I felt

like I lived in a palace. I had my own world up above the fray. The children felt far away yet safe. Moonbeams streamed through the crescent window and cast a silver streak across my bed.

I sighed happily. The divorce was behind me. We were in our own home. I was using my legal skills to help kids in need. Everything was finally coming together. Sleepily, I giggled, remembering my conversation with the guy who'd delivered the beds.

"Where does the queen go?" he'd held my mattress high.

"Third floor," I'd answered, pointing upstairs, "because that's where she lives."

Life was great.

IT WAS MONDAY and time to head to the camp bus. When I turned the van around to pull out of the driveway, Sammy still wasn't with us.

"Where's Sammy?" I asked.

"He's coming." Josh pointed to the side of the house.

Sammy ran toward us from the back, along the crushed-stone walkway on the side of the house. Large fieldstones bordered each side of the walkway. When he reached us, he slid open the rear door on the passenger side and popped into his seat.

"All set?" I asked, remembering that he'd done the same thing yesterday when we'd run a quick errand.

He nodded a preoccupied yes. I shifted into drive, and we were off. We made the bus in plenty of time.

I always waited with all the other moms until the bus left. We'd wave as it pulled away, but only the youngest campers waved back. The older ones were already busy with their friends. My friend Maureen's daughter was a rocket camper that year. That Monday, we stood together and gabbed while we waited.

I was dressed to unpack boxes: well-worn T-shirt, baggy shorts, and sneakers. Maureen was dressed—as she always is—for any occasion: groomed curly hair, color-coordinated clothes, fashionable but sensible shoes. It is never possible to tell if Maureen is on her way to chair a meeting or to shop for groceries.

"I wear a T-shirt and jeans when I garden," she claimed one day when I asked.

But I would not be surprised if she stood up from her flowers wearing a perfectly pressed pair of pants.

"How's it going with the move?" Maureen held a coffee in one hand; with the other she waved as the bus started to pull out.

"For some reason, Sammy won't use the front door"—I waved harder because I detected a slight motion coming from James—"but other than that, it's going well."

The bus pulled out of the parking lot, and we started walking back to our cars.

"How's your summer so far?" I asked.

"Good. Busy. I'm off to buy save-the-date cards for my son's bar mitzvah."

"Isn't that next summer?" I was puzzled. Sammy was in her son's Hebrew school class, and I thought they were both turning thirteen the following year.

"Never hurts to be early." She smiled.

Maureen is an overachiever. As best I can tell, her only flaw is that she does not kayak.

WHEN THE KIDS got home from camp, I was floating in a sea of corrugated cardboard. It had been a good day. I had managed to unpack more boxes, juggle a couple of calls, and take a quick kayak at high tide. Josh and James flopped down in front of the television. Sammy did his usual thing of grabbing a snack and heading outside to wander. I was so busy unpacking that I didn't notice much more about them. As long as they weren't complaining, I figured they were happy, but I took a break from the boxes and looked out the window when I heard Sammy screaming.

"SHUT UUUUP!!!" he was hollering at the treetops.

I had never heard him yell "Shut up" like that before. I made a mental note to speak to him, then went back to my boxes and promptly forgot.

Sammy opted to sleep in the den again that night. I was disappointed that he didn't want to stay in his room, but I knew it had something to do with grief over the move. I decided to let it go.

"It's chilly tonight. Do you want this?" I held out his favorite blanket, the tartan plaid.

"Just put it over there." He pointed to the other couch. "I'll get it later if I need it."

I COULD HAVE USED another week of rocket camp, but it would end on Friday. Then they'd be going off in three different directions, which meant I'd be doing a lot of driving. As hard as I worked to unpack that week, there were always more boxes. And I kept opening boxes full of things I didn't want: clothes they'd outgrown, broken toys, tennis balls that had lost their bounce. Why had I paid good money to move them? Most frustrating of all, Sammy's adjustment to the new house was not going well.

Camp was over an hour away, so making the bus was crucial. My kids had always been fast in the morning, but Sammy was slowing all of us down, like a piece of grit in a well-oiled machine. On Monday, I had casually wondered about him not using the front door, but it quickly became a permanent quirk.

On Tuesday, Josh and James and I dashed out the front. Sammy again bolted for the back. We sat in the van and watched him hop his way to us along the large fieldstones that bordered the walkway.

"What's he doing now?" I asked aloud to no one in particular.

"He's being annoying," said Josh.

Just as I rolled down the window to shout about hurrying, he fell off a fieldstone and ran the rest of way to the van.

"Sammy, why are you doing that?" I scolded when he jumped into the van. "You're making us late!"

"It makes it more interesting," he answered.

"Well, make it interesting after camp, not when we're trying to get there."

"Okay, Mom."

We pulled away.

On Wednesday, things got even more complicated. Sammy repeated his hopping on fieldstones to reach the front driveway, but each time he slipped off a stone, he ran back to the beginning to start again.

"Sammy! Get over here!" I shouted from the van.

I could not remember the last time Sammy had been disobedient. He'd always tried so hard to please, but not now. He kept hopping.

On Thursday, he held his breath while he hopped and ran.

"Sammy!" I yelled from the driver's seat. "We are going to miss the bus! GET IN THE VAN!"

He ignored me. His attention remained riveted on hopping the rugged fieldstones that bordered the walkway. He'd hop a few fieldstones, slip off onto the crushed-stone path, get back on the fieldstones, and repeat this behavior again and again. Finally, when he had hopped his way to the front without slipping off a fieldstone, he ran to the van and jumped in.

"Sorry, Mom."

We zoomed away.

On Friday, the last day of camp, I stood in the driveway at the side of the van and hollered for Sammy to hurry. He hopped, jumped, held his breath, slid off the fieldstones, raced back to the beginning, started again, slipped, repeated, and finally ran to the van with his body hunched over in the shape of an upside-down L. We caught the bus as it was pulling out of the parking lot. I flagged it down with my lights. It pulled to a stop, and I rushed the boys out. Sammy climbed out clumsily, jerked his way across the parking lot, then stopped midway and started spinning.

"What on earth is he doing now?" I wondered as I watched him spin his way onto the bus.

A WEEK PASSED. I was still unpacking. Sammy was still on the couch. I was exhausted from all the work and irritated by his lack of gratitude. I had worked hard to buy this house. I, too, was disappointed to leave the ocean, but our new place was great and the kids had all signed on for this move. It was time he got over it, began to like the new house, and started sleeping in his room. He'd spent only two nights there since the move.

Get with the program! I wanted to shout. I didn't, but I made my expectation clear.

"I want you sleeping in your room tonight," I said as he sat on the couch watching television.

"After this show," he answered.

In the morning, when I came downstairs, he was still on the couch.

On the few nights when he capitulated and went to his room, he refused to get into his bed. He slept on the floor, or sitting up in a chair at his desk.

"Don't you like your room?" I asked.

"It's fine, Mom." He looked away.

"Then what's the problem?"

No answer.

I tried putting a blow-up bed in my room.

"Sammy, come here," I called down from my room at ten one night.

He came upstairs holding his breath.

"What?" he asked on an exhalation.

"I made this up for you." I pointed at the plastic bed that I'd outfitted with fresh sheets and his tartan blanket. "You're sleeping there tonight."

He waited until he thought I was asleep; then he crawled off.

"Get back into the bed right now!" I barked, sitting up and pointing at it. He scurried back, waited a while, and then—like a cat—crept off. After five or six times, I gave up and let him go.

He hated the new house. He screamed at the squirrels. He pelted repairmen with acorns. He made a "camp" in the woods with a tattered flag and the mailbox we'd brought from our rental. He spent most of the day there and refused to go anywhere else. At night, he walked around inside the house until midnight, and then he collapsed on the couch.

I had expected that he might have a tough time with the move, but I'd had no idea it would be this bad. I tried things that might help get his mind off his grief. I drove him to the pier for ice cream. When we got there, he jumped out and started running back the way we'd come.

"Sammy, please get in the van," I pleaded through the window as I trailed him.

He kept running, all the way home.

Another day I drove him to the cove to search the tide pools, but he wouldn't leave the van. I thought he was too filled with grief to set foot on the sand.

Maybe exercise might help; I always felt better after I exercised.

"Let's take a bike ride; we'll go to the Candy Man," I suggested, adding the enticement of our local, old-fashioned sweet-shop.

"I hate bikes!" he screamed and ran back to his camp in the woods.

I tried him at golf camp.

The pro called. "Uh, apparently he doesn't like golf. I think you better come get him."

"It's the move," I told the puzzled pro when I arrived to retrieve Sammy. "We're in a new house, and he misses the old one."

Sammy stood at the side of the course, sobbing.

"Use the front door!" I yelled at Sammy when we got back. "I mean it. You come in this door right now!" I was furious. This had gone on long enough.

Sammy held his breath and ran in through the front. He raced across the first floor and darted out the back door. Once outside, he started all the nutty stuff again, the hopping, yelling, and spinning.

I watched with a sick feeling in the pit of my stomach.

He came through the back door after a good hour with tears in his eyes. "Mom," he cried, "did you ever notice how you're seeing a psychiatrist when you don't need to and then when you need to, you're not?"

Sammy did not know the difference between a psychiatrist (who can prescribe medicine) and a psychologist (who can only offer counseling services). But I knew he was referring to the child psychologist he'd seen briefly in third grade when I thought he might be having emotional issues. The sessions ended when I'd realized that what he actually needed was a different reading program.

I called the child psychologist immediately and set up an appointment for the following week. This psychologist had also helped Josh through the earliest years of my separation from his dad. I set up four appointments. A month of good, solid counseling would take care of Sammy's anxiety about the move.

"Sammy," I said to comfort him, "it's the stress. We have a lot going on. You'll go in, talk things over, and it will get better. Don't worry." I told him this while he ate standing up, at the end of the table, with his eyes open only to slits. It had been over a week since he'd been willing to sit at the table. And then I tried to hug him.

"Don't touch me!" he screamed, dropping the slice of watermelon he'd been holding. He ran downstairs and out the back door. "You made it worse!" he yelled as he ran to his camp in the woods.

I stood on the second-story porch, sick to my stomach, listening to his sobs and screams as they carried across the woods. I wondered when I'd be able to hug him again.

THE NEXT DAY, Josh was going to play cards at a shop in Portland with his and Sammy's friend Devers. The shop had Magic tournaments, and Sammy wanted to go, too. It was one of their favorite games. This was a good sign. *The grief must be waning*, I thought.

Sammy had known Devers since kindergarten. He and Devers had attended a special math class for gifted children at the grade school. Rocket camp had solidified their friendship, and Josh liked Devers, too. The plan was for me to get them to the card shop. Devers's mom, Chris, would get them home.

Chris called after they'd been there for about an hour.

"Beth, something's wrong. I'm at the shop, and Sammy's crying. He won't stop."

"Oh no." I let out a defeated sigh. "Did anything happen?"

"Nope. Everything was good, and suddenly he started crying. Listen."

Chris held the phone away from her ear. I could hear Sammy wailing in the background.

"Hear that?" She was back on the line. "I'm very concerned."

"He's just still so upset that we moved. Can you get him to talk to me?" I asked.

"Not sure," she said.

I heard her ask Sammy if he'd talk to me; then she was back on the line again.

"He won't come to the phone," she said.

"Let me talk to Josh."

"Okay, hold on. Here he is." There was the jumble of a phone changing hands.

"It's that crying thing again, Mom," Josh said, "but I think he's okay now. It's the same thing he's been doing at home."

"Does he want to come home? I can come get him, and you can stay with Devers."

"Sammy, do you want Mom to come get you?" Josh called out, then came back on the line. "He says no."

"Let me talk to Chris again." Josh passed the phone.

"I think I should come get him," I told her.

"I'm not sure about that," she said. "He's going inside now. Yup, he's inside and going over to the table. He looks like he wants to play."

"I think I should come." I searched for my keys.

"I'm watching him through the window, and he's picked up some cards. He really looks okay. How about I'll call you if it gets bad again?"

I thought things over. Maybe playing Magic might help with his grief.

"All right," I said, "but call right away."

"I will," she said, and we hung up.

Chris brought the boys home a few hours later. Sammy got out of the car and ran, hunched over, to the walkway.

"What do you make of that?" I asked Chris as we watched him hop the fieldstones and head for the back.

"I'd be very concerned."

I did not know Chris very well, but I liked her. She had shoulder-length blond hair and clear blue eyes that projected intelligence and intensity. Chris was trained as a speech therapist, and she often helped at the grade school by working with special needs children. I was touched by her concern over my son.

"I've got him set up for counseling, and I gotta figure he'll get better. I think it's because of all the added stress from moving. With Josh going away and Sammy starting middle school, I guess it's too much for him. I'm beginning to think the move was a mistake."

"All this from moving?" she asked.

"I don't know what else it could be." We stood quietly for a minute and watched Sammy disappear around the back of the house.

I WAS AT MY desk the following day when I heard loud pounding coming from the second floor. I ran downstairs and screamed. Sammy was banging his head against the sliding glass door.

"Sammy! Stop! Stop!" I yelled.

"I can't!" he sobbed. "It's like a mental itch!"

WE FAITHFULLY ATTENDED each counseling session. Sammy dutifully got in the van, and I drove to the psychologist's office. At each session, I would spend five or ten minutes bringing the psychologist up to date about the preceding week. This would consist of my describing what new and bizarre behaviors had developed.

"Why isn't he getting better?" I asked, first politely and, later, more sharply. "Can stress really cause all this?"

"Let me talk to him and see if I can find out more," the psychologist answered. "Try not to focus on it too much."

Then Sammy would go in and speak with the psychologist for the rest of the session. I left with no answers. The conversation on the car ride home was always the same.

"How was it, Sammy?" I'd ask.

"Fine," he'd answer.

"Is it helping?"

"I don't know," he'd say curtly.

Sammy grew worse. He snorted and puffed and gasped for breath. He wanted us to be perfectly still and quiet. I reported these newest behaviors at the sessions and still heard nothing definitive. Privately, I thought the sessions seemed like a waste of time, but I told myself to give the process more time. I was not a patient person. I knew that about myself, and I wanted to do right by my son.

Then Sammy stopped sleeping. He paced all night, faster and faster. Sometimes he ran. His feet boomed as he dashed from the second floor to the first and back again.

"Please, Sammy, go to bed," I begged at three in the

morning when the noise woke me up. The house was blazing, with every light turned on, and I tried to turn them off.

"Leave me alone!" he yelled as he fought me for control of the switches.

We sweltered in the August heat because all the windows had to be shut. If we opened one, to catch just a moment of breeze, he screamed as if he'd been lashed with a whip.

After three sessions with the psychologist and no improvement, I was desperate. The doctor was quiet and patient.

"Don't you think we need to be more concerned?" I demanded.

"Only if it's interfering with the home." The doctor stroked his beard.

Had I not described things clearly? In one short month, our lives had been turned upside down.

"How could it not be interfering with the home?" I strained to be polite. "He doesn't sleep. He doesn't eat. Every light has to be on twenty-four/seven. All the windows have to be shut. He screams at us if we breathe too loudly. Every day it's something new. There has to be something going on here other than stress."

"Let's wait another week," he said carefully.

"One week," I repeated. I thought for a moment. I hated to overreact. I did not want to be a hysterical mother. I wanted to stay logical and focused and clear.

"I'm taking Josh up to boarding school this weekend; if he's not better by the time I get back, we need to do something more."

New behaviors continued to come at a fever pitch. Sammy

stopped using his hands; then they shrunk up into his sleeves. He used the top of his head to flick light switches. He opened doors with his forearms and closed them with his legs.

"Open it! Open it!" he'd stand at the door and cry when he couldn't get the handle to turn with his limbs.

He stopped bathing and changing his clothes. He slithered his entire body along the side of the wall, like a dog that needed scratching.

The drive to Josh's boarding school was coming up. The trip would be a half day each way. I canceled the sitter I'd engaged to stay with Sammy and James. There was no way I could leave Sammy behind. I would not let him out of my sight.

"Please, Mom, let me stay here alone!" he shrieked while Josh and I packed Josh up for school.

I shook my head no and kept packing.

OUR GOOD-BYE CELEBRATION DINNER plans had lost their appeal. I suggested that we cancel the restaurant and opt for takeout instead. Sammy insisted that we go.

It was the end of August, and the weather was hot and humid. Except for Sammy, there was not a person in the whole town wearing long sleeves and pants. He wore the same clothes he had put on the last time he had changed, a week or so ago, maybe longer. Between unpacking from the move, repacking for Josh, trying to work, and being sleep-deprived, my nerves wrecked over Sammy, I had lost track of just about everything— maybe even my own sanity.

Alisson's was the kids' favorite restaurant. We were seated at one of the round tables just off the bar. The waitress brought the bread. I propped my head on my hand and tried to stay awake. I took a piece of bread and, with bleary eyes, looked at the napkin that poked out from Sammy's sleeve. Somewhere up there was his hand, shrunken to the shape of a claw. He had started using napkins or tissues to hold things ever since his hand had disappeared.

Sammy reached for the bread with the napkin. With his right arm extended, out came the claw. His sleeve pulled back about three inches above his wrist. I caught sight of the lower part of his forearm and sucked in my breath. It was entirely black-and-blue! I reached across the table, grabbed the claw, and pushed the sleeve up above his elbow. His entire right arm was one big nasty mass of bruises. I got up from the chair and grabbed the other arm. He tried to get away, but I held him tight and pushed up the sleeve. The left arm was black-and-blue! I grabbed hold of his legs and pushed up his pant legs while he wriggled and cried. Both legs were in Technicolor.

"My God, Sammy!" I gasped as I pulled up his shirt. His entire torso was bruised! The odd ways he had been using his torso and limbs had caused all these bruises. He was screaming and struggling to get away.

"I just wanted to be normal!" he yelled and sobbed. "Just one normal night with everyone! Why did you do this? Why did you do this to me? Couldn't you leave me alone just this once?"

A hushed silence fell over the restaurant, while the other patrons stared.

I DO NOT REMEMBER finishing dinner or driving home or whether I slept that night. What I do remember is lying in my bed, alone and scared to death. I listened to my darling son pound and snort his way around the house. When I got up to try to help, it made things worse. He cried and screamed at me to leave him alone. I hurried back upstairs, lay helplessly in my bed, and cursed myself for being so stupid as to buy this house.

The next day we left to take Josh to boarding school.

The day after that, Sammy ran away.

3

The Runaway

Northern and southern Maine, like their counterparts in California, each have a distinctly different feel. In Maine, the dividing line is Bangor, about midway up the state. The last big shopping mall is in Bangor. North of that, the pace changes. The busy south gives way to a land full of wildlife, potato farms, paper mills, and mountains. The conventional wisdom says that a politician can come from the north and succeed in the south, but not the other way around. The Mainers of the southern coast, so close to Boston, are almost from a different state. While most of southern Maine focuses on tomorrow, most of northern Maine is comfortably rooted in its deep traditions and how it's always been.

Sometimes, how it was is better.

IT WAS THE LONGEST, most agonizing car ride of my life. We left southern Maine at midday and drove north. Josh was in the passenger seat beside me. Sammy was behind us in the middle seat on the passenger side. James was in the bench seat at the back. Josh's school was in Limestone, just one mile from the Canadian border. It would be dark when we arrived, and I was anxious. Dark in rural Maine is different. There are no streetlights or stoplights or other human illuminations to guide the way. The night sky can be so black that the silhouettes of trees are not visible. Without a clear sky and a brilliant moon, there is no help beyond a driver's headlights. Even in daylight, the terrain is rough and demanding.

I spent most of the long drive glancing over my shoulder at Sammy. I was sick with worry. He had pushed himself into the corner of his seat, hunched over, and refused to use a seat belt. Asking what I could do to help only made it worse.

"I'm *fine*," he growled through clenched teeth.

I watched through the windshield as southern Maine dovetailed into the rugged north. We passed lumber mills, Moose Crossing signs, and Mount Katahdin. I wondered about the stress theory. Could that really be the cause?

Endless acres spilled out in either direction, structures dwindled, a bear lumbered across the road. The landscape became desolate, and everything looked the same. Lots of wrong turns later, I finally found the hotel. Josh and James bounded out of the van.

"Try to get us started with the registration," I told Josh.

He nodded and went in. James followed.

Sammy tried to get out of the van, but he couldn't. Each time he put a foot on the running board, he turned back inside, sat down, rocked back and forth, and then tried again.

"What can I do to help?" I asked.

He did not answer.

In, out, in, out: we were there for fifteen minutes. Finally, once out for good, he walked forward then backward, spun in circles, jumped, twitched, and pounded his way to the lobby. After an agonizing half hour, he hopped into the room. Josh and James were already settled in. It was late, and they went right to sleep.

Sammy sat bolt upright on the floor and refused to move. I begged him to get into a bed and sleep. He ignored me and sat there, straight as an arrow, all night. I'd drift off for a bit, wake up, plead with him, drift off, and then repeat the surreal scene again.

The next day was a dreary gray. Josh was impatient to get going, but Sammy would not leave the room. He spun and scratched and rubbed his feet back and forth on the carpet. He clenched his eyes. He held his ears shut with fingertips while he huffed and puffed.

"I—want—to—stay—here," he pushed out between breaths.

"We've checked out, Sammy. No one can stay."

Once I got him to the van, he repeated his in-and-out routine. By the time he finally sat down and we could leave, it was late.

"It's my day, and he's ruining it!" Josh exploded.

"He's sick, Josh. Something's wrong," I answered.

I got lost driving to the school and could not find a single place to stop for directions or person to ask for help. Eventually, I flagged down the one car that was traveling on the same empty road. The driver pointed us in the right direction. We pulled up late for registration. Josh, fuming, went in alone. I stayed in the van with Sammy and James. I angled my rearview mirror so that I could watch Sammy without craning my neck. Looking through the windshield, I took in the surroundings.

There were two brick buildings: an older one, which housed the classrooms, and a modern structure, which housed the dorms. Both buildings rested at the base of a hill; behind them were acres of barren landscape that stretched farther than I could see. Playing fields were stamped into the acres. Forests bordered the far end of the fields. Separating the playing fields from the vastness beyond was a chain-link fence.

All around us, in a crush of excitement, parents and students carried boxes and suitcases and crates into the dorm. They happily shouted instructions back and forth. Josh came back with the key to his room and flipped open the back of the van. He pulled out a suitcase and headed into the dorm. I was scared to leave Sammy, but Josh needed help.

"Stay here!" I ordered. I grabbed a box and hurried in after Josh.

I dropped the box in Josh's room and said a quick hello to his roommate's parents.

"Are you coming to the parents' orientation?" they asked.

"Probably not," I tossed over my shoulder as I ran back to the van.

Both boys were there. I grabbed another box, dropped it in Josh's room, and rushed back out. When I got there, James was alone.

"Where's Sammy?" My heart jumped into my throat.

James looked up lazily from his Game Boy. "He said to tell you that you couldn't give him what he needed, so he had to take care of it himself."

"Which way did he go?" I shouted.

James pointed toward the thousands of empty acres.

"SAMMY!" I screamed and ran up the closest hill.

I crisscrossed open acres, breathless and panicked, while hollering Sammy's name. I ran as fast and far as I possibly could, with no idea where I was going. The van became a speck behind me. Eventually, I stopped from sheer exhaustion and slowly turned around in a complete circle. There was nothing and no one in sight—just endless acres, the woods, and, beyond that, rolling mountains. I was Julie Andrews in a horror version of *The Sound of Music.*

"SAMMY!" I screamed in every direction. Silence was the reply.

In the distance, I saw James coming up the hill.

"Go back!" I shouted through hands cupped like a megaphone, then pointed at the van.

If Sammy was hiding in the fields, there was no chance I would find him. I envisioned search teams and helicopters and news crews set up on the hills. I shut that image out. I knew my son and trusted my instincts. He did not head for the woods. He had probably doubled back to the town below. If I hurried, I might catch him. I raced down the hill for the van. James was already there.

I drove up and down the streets of Limestone, searching with my eyes and my heart. I combed the main street first, then the residential streets, one by one. Suddenly, I spotted a strange motion in a parking lot, behind an old, two-story, wooden apartment building. Sammy looked like an exaggerated toy soldier. His clenched fists and thrashing arms jerked up and down from his elbows. The top of his body was rigid, but his whole body shook from the motion of his arms. I careened into the parking lot and slammed on the brakes. He saw me and took off up the street at a run.

"Stay here!" I hollered at James. In one motion, I jumped out of the van, onto broken pieces of pavement, and started racing after Sammy. I caught up to him half a block away and grabbed him around the waist and held tight. He screamed and kicked.

"You have to get in the van!" I shouted over his screams. He fought harder to get away. He punched and scratched. I pulled and dragged him back to the van. I tried to shove him through the door. He was smaller than I, but he used his legs to block the way. I could not wedge him through.

He wriggled loose and ran again. I chased and caught him halfway up a hilly street. I locked my right arm around his shoulders. He struggled, but I held on tight. We ran together up the hill while he pulled and tried to get away. We shouted to each other as we ran.

"I'm running away!" he screamed.

"You'll never get rid of me!" I shouted back. "I'm like the mother in *The Runaway Bunny*." Maybe, I thought, if I reminded him of the book we'd read when he was little, he would listen.

"I'm leaving!" He was crying.

"Please, baby, come back."

"No!"

"You've got an appointment with the doctor tomorrow. We'll figure out what's wrong. I promise. I love you, Sammy! You must get in the van!" I spotted a police station farther up the road. If I had to, I'd pull him there.

"No! I'm not coming with you." He would not listen. He kept trying to get away.

"The state might take you. You're black-and-blue! They'll think I hit you. They might take Josh and James, too. They could send you all away from me!"

Abruptly, he stopped. Then he turned completely around and walked quickly back down the hill. I turned with him. My right arm remained locked firmly around his shoulders. At the van, he stepped onto the running board and got in without hesitating. I flicked the child locks, hoping to confine him, slid the door shut, and climbed into the driver's seat. Every inch of me was shaking.

"How did this happen?" I sobbed, gulping for air.

4

Diagnosis

On a day in late August when a storm has cleared and a rainbow paints the sky, I grab my paddle and head for the seals. They rest on their backs, their noses poked high, while they float and drift with the tide. Their bellies are full, their whiskers distinguished and dripping beyond their chins. They peer as I pass. Their eyes look like glass, and they stare at me cautiously. The seals all know instinctively what men have learned over time: the best salt-water fishing in Maine comes when August folds into fall.

The striped bass are heading south by then—and so were we.

IF THE RIDE UP to Limestone was the worst car ride of my life, the trip back was a living hell. Sammy was crunched into the corner of his seat. The clawed thumbs of his empty hands moved back and forth as if he held a Game Boy. His head bobbed with the bumps in the road. I couldn't tell if his eyes were open or shut. I just knew that he was far away.

My mind was spinning. When did he last eat? Why didn't I know this? What kind of mother was I? Maybe if I'd served him a decent meal instead of working so hard, none of this would have happened.

"Sammy, should we stop and get something to eat?" I called back periodically to him. He did not give me a response.

"I'm hungry, Mom," James answered instead.

"Where are those pretzels I brought with us?"

"We ate them," James answered.

"Are there any apples left?"

"Yes."

"Eat those."

I thought about Sammy standing at the table during meal after meal, with his eyes shut. Had he actually eaten? I had been in overdrive for weeks. In addition to the packing, the unpacking, and all the craziness around Sammy, one of my clients was closing a major deal. I had been pushing that deal through night and day. Had I neglected my child because of my work? Was it my fault this had happened?

"Sammy, do you want to stop for food?" I called back again much later. Still no response.

Stress isn't causing Sammy's problems! my head and my heart shouted silently together.

IT WAS TEN O'CLOCK by the time we got home that night. I readied myself to dash through the woods if he bolted when I parked, but he did not move. I woke James, held his soft cheeks in my hands, and spoke into his ear.

"You are to go directly into the house and up to bed. Do you understand me?" I spoke in a low, commanding-officer kind of voice. "Right into your room and shut your door."

"But I'm hungry," James whined softly.

"Get an apple and take it into your room; that's the best we can do tonight."

James nodded and headed for the house.

I watched James go inside; then I turned to Sammy. He was hunched over into a ball in his seat. He nodded: yes, he would come into the house. He shook his head: no, he would not run away. I followed him around to the back of the house, and we went in. I locked every door, turned on every light, and shut every window. Once confined, I knew, he would not leave, since he would not touch a door handle. I left him on the first floor in the den; then I went up to my office. I called the psychologist's voice mail and left a detailed message about what had happened.

"This is not stress," I said through gritted teeth. "There is something medically wrong."

Then I typed a fax to the pediatrician describing what was going on and telling him that I needed a call back first thing in the morning with an appointment time. I noted that we were in an urgent, life-threatening situation and I needed his help. Then I collapsed on my bed and listened to Sammy pound his way around the house.

I called the pediatrician at 9:01 the next morning. The nurse answered. I held while she searched for the fax and went to talk to the doctor; then she came back on and delivered the news.

"The doctor says you should take him to the crisis unit."

"Are you saying the doctor won't see my son?" I felt the hairs stand up on the back of my neck.

"He says you should go to the crisis unit," she repeated.

"I think we have a misunderstanding here," I said slowly. "Sammy has been the doctor's patient for more than five years. He is sick. He needs to see his doctor. We are going to be at the psychologist's office at three P.M. Right after that, I will walk him over to see the doctor. If four o'clock isn't good, tell me another time, and we'll be there." She put me on hold again; then she came back on the line.

"He says you should take him to the crisis unit," she repeated once more.

"So you're saying he refuses to see my son?" I asked, my blood boiling over.

"He thinks you need the crisis unit," she said.

"Without even seeing him," I stated.

I had been a guardian *ad litem* long enough to know that the crisis unit is the last place you take your child. It is absolutely the very last place. You take your child to the crisis unit when you are totally and completely out of options, when you have tried everything else and you have absolutely nowhere else to go. It is the last stop on a dead end. The crisis unit is where I visit the children who are out of control and suicidal or homicidal, the kids who are hallucinating, the kids whose parents have beaten them so badly that they start a fire to burn down the house. It's where you'll find the thirteen-year-old girls who have group sex with a dozen grown men because they've been molested or abandoned and they feel so lousy about themselves they think maybe this will help. It's where the kids learn from one another how to cut themselves. My son was not going to the crisis unit. He did not need a holding cell disguised as a hospital. He needed a medical doctor to figure out what was wrong with him, and his own doctor would not see him.

Sammy's pediatrician was fired the moment he refused to see my son, but I was not going to say that until I had his replacement lined up.

"Tell him thanks for me, will you?" I said and hung up the telephone.

Later that day, we went to see the psychologist. Sammy waited skittishly in the lobby while I met with the psychologist. I was dangerously close to screaming that I felt he had wasted our time, but I mustered all of my self-control.

"We've got one minute," I told him, seething, "because he might run away. We're not waiting any longer to see if he gets better. This isn't stress. There is something terribly wrong, and I want my kid back. His doctor has refused to see him, and these sessions are doing nothing. Where do we go from here?"

He gave me a list of about a dozen child psychiatrists. "Tell them we need a screen out for obsessive-compulsive disorder—OCD," he said.

I went back to the lobby and breathed a sigh of relief, because Sammy was still there. He went into the office. They spoke briefly, and then we went home.

I made calls relentlessly to all the doctors on the list. I could not reach any of them. I left messages, and most did not call back. Those who did call—usually days after I had left my urgent message—said it would be about three months before I could get an appointment.

"In three months, he could be dead," I told one of them.

"And if I did see him," noted another, "it would only be to give a diagnosis. I don't do treatment."

I could not find a single psychiatrist in all of southern Maine who would see my son.

I BRIEFLY THOUGHT there was hope when Sammy asked one day if there were some type of drink I could get him. He said he couldn't eat anything, but that a drink made with fruit would be good. Watermelon was his favorite fruit.

"Watermelon in the blender?" I asked excitedly.

"Whatever you want," he answered as I hurried off to the kitchen.

When I handed him the glass, he held it high in the air.

"To new beginnings," Sammy said as he chugged it.

I thought that all might be well; maybe he'd eat again.

He did not get well; he got worse. He relentlessly rubbed, paced, huffed, puffed, and held his breath. We were not allowed to look at him. One night he caught me watching him. He screamed and cried for an hour.

Sometimes at one or two in the morning, Sammy would finally go into his room. On the first night this happened, when he slammed his door and all the sounds stopped, I crept quietly down the stairs. I lay on the floor outside his room, listening for sounds that might mean he was trying to hurt himself. All was quiet, so I tried to open the door, but it wouldn't budge. I tried to look under the crack at the bottom of the door, but it was too thin. I went outside and set up a ladder to his second-story window. I could see him on the floor, curled in a fetal position, pushed up against the door. He was breathing. He was safe. After that, when his door slammed late at night and the sounds quieted, I came downstairs and slept on the floor outside his room.

I sent James to my parents in New Jersey, and I cried all the way home from the airport. I had no choice. I was unable to do anything except try to take care of Sammy. Some nights I would wake from my place on the floor and go lie on James's bed, sobbing, because I missed him so much. I wanted my baby with me.

I wasted precious days making useless calls to psychiatrists in Maine. I waited for return calls that never came and finally expanded my search to New Hampshire. It was there I found Dr. Drill. His office called me right back, but—once again—there was no availability. In fact, his receptionist explained, he had canceled all his appointments because his wife was over-due with their first child.

"So he has no patients this week?"

"That's correct," she answered.

"But he's in the office?"

"Yes."

"Suppose we make an appointment and understand that he'll cancel if she goes into labor? If you call and we're on our way, we'll turn back."

There was silence on the other end of the line.

"Please," I begged. "My son is desperately ill, and I can't find anyone in Maine to see him. I'll pay cash. We can be there on two hours' notice."

She hesitated, then said, "Hold on."

I prayed while I waited, and then she came back on the line.

"Tomorrow at two, but he might have to cancel."

"I know. Thank you. Thank him for me. Thank you so much."

The next day we were in Portsmouth, New Hampshire. I watched Sammy in Dr. Drill's waiting room as he held his ears shut, huffed and puffed, and rubbed his feet back and forth on the rug. His clothes were rumpled and filthy. His eyes were like slits. He hopped. He pounded. He did everything but shriek. He bore no resemblance whatsoever to the award-winning, kindhearted, brilliant son who had been mine just six weeks before. I did not recognize this child.

"I'm fine," Sammy sneered at anyone who expressed concern, asking if they could help or get him anything.

I saw the staff whispering. I knew it was about him. The receptionist was so alarmed that she made Dr. Drill begin our appointment early. Sammy snorted and huffed his way from the reception area to Dr. Drill's office. He scraped his body along the wall. It took him about ten minutes to cover a distance that would usually take less than a minute. Once in the office, Sammy was theoretically "on" the leather couch. In reality: he was squirming, turning sideways, snaking along the cushions, hanging his legs over the back, rubbing his body on the side arms of the couch, squinting his eyes, holding his ears shut, and gasping for breath.

The office had a large desk, Oriental rugs, a leather couch, and two leather chairs that faced the couch. The walls were lined with bookcases full of complicated titles. I sat on one of the leather chairs, trying hard to appear calm and responsible, even though I wanted to scream. The doctor faced us from the other chair. He was trim with dark hair. Dr. Drill may have been the only doctor who would see Sammy, but he had excellent credentials and was extremely well respected. We were in good hands.

"What seems to be the problem, Sammy?" Dr. Drill asked as he watched my son through his black-framed glasses.

Sammy wriggled around violently on the couch. "Why don't you ask my mother? She's the one who thinks I need to be here." He pushed the words out, in the middle of snorting, while he glared at the doctor.

"It started about six weeks ago," I said quietly, "and here's what is happening now." I reached into my bag and retrieved a sheet of typing paper. I had anticipated that this question would come in one form or another. I thought it might be too painful to detail the behaviors in front of Sammy, so I had compiled the long list at home. It included all of the behaviors I had spoken about with the psychologist and his newest ones, too: scratching and picking at his skin, blowing on his hands, constantly pulling at his clothes as if they were too tight.

"Yesterday," I added as I handed the list to Dr. Drill, "we had to take all the clocks off the walls and put them in closets because he can't stand the ticking."

The doctor and I talked about the list while Sammy, on his back, skidded from one end of the couch to the other. Then the doctor asked Sammy if he had any questions.

"Yes." He squinted and slithered. "Did you wear a pocket protector in high school?"

"No," answered Dr. Drill, who seemed somewhat uncomfortable.

I sat there and wondered what a pocket protector was.

We sent Sammy out. I knew that because of Sammy's strange behaviors, it would take him at least ten minutes to reach the reception area; that gave me ten private minutes with the doctor to find out what on earth was wrong with my son. He gave me the diagnosis the psychologist had suspected: obsessive-compulsive disorder, commonly known as OCD.

"His behaviors are compulsions," the doctor explained. "They are beyond his control."

"You're saying he can't stop himself from doing any of this?" It was a tough concept to register.

"That's right." Dr. Drill thumbed the pages of a prescription pad.

The doctor said it had to do with something called serotonin. Sammy's brain was making serotonin but absorbing it into his system too quickly. He had a chemical imbalance, and medication could help with that. The dose would start small and then increase as his body became able to process the dose more quickly. We wanted the medication to stay in his system and slow things down, so we would periodically increase the dose.

"But where did this come from?" I asked. "Six weeks ago he was fine."

"Sometimes it happens like that," the doctor answered, searching for a pen.

"With no family history?" I asked.

"There's probably an uncle out there, or another relative who was odd, but no one talks about it." He scribbled on the pad.

"I don't think so." I shook my head and carefully searched my memory. It came up blank.

"You're in for a long haul ahead," the doctor said and handed me a prescription.

"How long will it take for him to get better?" I fingered the slip of paper on which all our hopes now rested.

He stood up and pulled a videotape from the bookcase be-hind him, then turned to face me.

"Sometimes the children get better." He hesitated. "And sometimes they don't." He added the last part quietly and proffered the videotape. It was called *Understanding Obsessive-Compulsive Disorder.*

"Thank you, Doctor." I took the tape and looked him square in the eyes. "My son will get better."

5

Fall

September brings big changes to Kennebunkport. The tourists leave. The traffic grows lighter. Crisp mornings yield to warm days. Flocks of monarch butterflies rest to feed on the yellow and violet flowers that line the rocky coast. Sea lavender blooms in the marsh. Canada geese fly victory signs across the sky. Wild turkeys are often seen in the fields, and the mice contemplate warmer homes.

There are fewer boats on the water; more seals poke their heads up to bathe in the quiet sun. It is the best time for eating and catching lobsters in Maine. The shells are harder, and the meat is juicy. The lobstermen are happy because their traps are full. On lucky nights, when the tide is high and the air is humid, a stream of brilliant white streaks a path across the black sea and up to a full moon.

At the crack of dawn, the big yellow buses roll, carting reluctant students off to school. Parents line the streets, holding the hands of the littlest ones and keeping an eye on the ones who feel they are old enough to be there alone. Kindergartners look forward to picking end-of-the-season blueberries on their first field trip. On weekends and afternoons, the soccer fields are full of parents and players. The trees are green, and the grass is lush. Football season is under way. Cross-country runners stretch their muscles. Local golfers fill the courses. Cyclists begin to wear long-sleeved jerseys.

Toward the end of the month, wisps of brown float down on a breeze and land on the ground. Fall is coming.

Sammy did not start back to school that September; he started Zoloft instead.

ZOLOFT IS A SELECTIVE serotonin reuptake inhibitor, an SSRI. All of the SSRIs try to slow down chemical processes in the brain. Serotonin is the brain chemical that gives people a sense of well-being. It is released and absorbed back into the brain through tiny nerve endings in a repetitive, split-second process. If things went as planned, and the medicine worked, it would cause serotonin to remain in Sammy's brain for longer periods. He'd feel better. Less anxiety would mean fewer obsessions and compulsions because OCD thrives on anxiety.

OCD floods its victim with obsessive thoughts and behaviors. The behaviors are called "compulsions" and are guided by various rules. A rule might be an absolute (do not touch a faucet), dictate a specific number of times the compulsion must be performed (slam the door four times), or require that the compulsion be performed in a certain place or ritualized fashion (close your eyes while eating and sit only at the end of the table). There are consequences if a rule is broken (reopen the door eight times, then repeat the compulsion).

Children with OCD are sometimes perceived as having discipline problems, so it's important to understand about the rules. The rules are the supreme authority, and breaking them is not an option. Children with OCD are not being willful or obstinate when they fail to comply with adult direction; they simply can't. They must follow the rules.

Sometimes OCD is manageable, but in its most debilitating form—which we faced with Sammy—the victim is so dominated by obsessions, compulsions, and rules that daily life becomes impossible.

"YOU'VE GOT A SEROTONIN issue," I told Sammy on the ride back from Dr. Drill's office.

I dropped the prescription off at Colonial Pharmacy as we passed through Dock Square on our way home. Colonial is located right on the square, in the center of Kennebunkport.

"He's very sick, Gary," I told the pharmacist as I placed the prescription on the counter. My eyes welled with tears. "I'll come back for it when I've got him settled."

I also made a quick stop at Bradbury's, the local seaside market. I wanted watermelon in case Sammy would eat. Bradbury's has everything from gourmet meat to the *New York Times,* and a post office is located right inside. A person could never venture beyond Bradbury's and still be fully informed and well fed. Many of the summer people do all their food shopping at Bradbury's. Locals use Bradbury's to fill in the gaps. At Bradbury's, I sometimes dash in still wearing my wet suit.

On this particular day, I was well dressed, having just been at the psychiatrist's office. I ran into Bradbury's, charged a watermelon to my account, and ran back out. Then I backed the van slowly out of the space and carefully started to pull around the back of the store to leave.

"Noooooooooooo!!!" Sammy screamed.

"What?" I yelled, slamming on the brakes, terrified that I'd hit someone.

"You have to go that way, back in and out again." He pointed frantically from our parking space to the parking lot entrance.

I tried to understand what he meant.

"In, then out again, that way!" He kept pointing from the space to the entrance.

"You mean backward?" I asked.

He nodded yes.

I sighed and grudgingly pulled the van back into the parking space, then sat for a minute with my hand on the gearshift.

I heard again the doctor's voice saying that some kids never get better. I thought about all the things I had changed in my life for Sammy. I thought about the friends I hadn't seen since June, and the kayaking I had missed this summer. I thought about sleeping night after night on the floor by his room and sending James away. I thought about having finally gotten my life together only to be saddled with an incredibly ill child. I saw my life unfurl as a giant ball and chain. I thought about how sick and tired I was of being a responsible, hardworking adult and parenting three sons on my own. I was angry and resentful, and I wanted to scream my head off. Instead, I heard a deep voice rise up from my gut.

"Let me tell you something, and you listen good and hard,"

I heard the voice say to Sammy. "This is the only time I will *ever* do something like this. If you want to hop on stones and hold your breath and repeat things again and again, you do it. But I will *never* do something like this again. Do you understand me?"

He nodded quickly.

I wanted to strangle him; then I wanted to strangle myself for being so unforgiving. I put the van into reverse and retraced our path, backward, as if running a movie in reverse.

DR. DRILL SAID it would take about two weeks for the medicine to begin to work. I optimistically made plans for James to come home. It would be good to have him back and in school, the first step of establishing a normal routine again. The two weeks passed without much improvement, but I did not change my plan.

Just a bit longer, I thought confidently.

James smiled and waved as he walked off the plane. The flight attendant delivered him into my arms. I scooped him up and held tight.

"Is Sammy better?" he asked right away.

"Not yet, but soon; we're waiting for the medicine to work."

James was excited because I was taking him directly to Consolidated School. His third-grade class was at recess, so we walked around to the field in the back. When his classmates saw him, they stopped their game of kickball and barreled over. They hollered his name and tackled him with bear hugs.

"Bye, Mom!" James shouted, waving over his shoulder as he raced off with his friends.

I stood at the side, watched, and remembered. Sammy had been like that once.

SAMMY WAS IN THE house with me all day while we waited for the Zoloft to take effect. I now understood that he had no choice but to engage in the bizarre behaviors. Attorney friends stepped in to cover my court appearances. I figured that he'd be better soon and completely recovered by Thanksgiving. He saw the psychologist once a week to help cope with his anxiety. Since transitioning to middle school might be part of the problem, I took him back to Consolidated to see his former teachers. Perhaps they might offer him comfort.

Nestled between soccer fields and hills for sledding, Consolidated School is one of the most caring places on earth. It is the heart of Kennebunkport. Everyone knows everyone else and their children. There are ice cream socials and Friday morning meetings. There are craft fairs and Halloween parties and spring recitals. It is a community.

"Come with me to Consolidated, Sammy. We'll see your old teachers. It might help."

My broken son forced himself into the van, and off we drove. My friend Carly was picking up her daughter, Abby, when I pulled in to park. Abby and James had been in nursery school together.

THREE OF MY CLOSEST friendships—with Carly, Tracy, and Marty—were forged when we were all moms at the same nursery school.

Carly and I had connected immediately because we both grew up in New Jersey. She had that South Jersey way: quick, sharp, very bottom-line. She was taking a break from teaching English until her kids were older. When Josh was in fifth grade,

Carly helped me by tutoring him in writing. Carly and I often took a quick morning kayak while the children were at nursery school during those years.

"Hold the boat still and listen to the quiet," she'd said one day back then.

Tracy had the most children of anyone in our group: two boys and two girls. Her youngest, Harrison, was in James's class. Before they were born, she had moved to the States from England. Tracy knew I was a bit of a news junkie and had deftly suggested that the evening news should be renamed *All America, All the Time*. She was always willing to help out by looking after her friends' children. Consequently, they happily spilled from her doorway, raced tricycles up and down her private lane, and bounced around on her trampoline. With her British accent and house full of rambunctious children, I thought of *Harry Potter* and the Weasleys whenever I pulled up.

Marty was pregnant with her second child when James and her first, Helen, attended nursery school together. Marty was the part-time librarian at the Cape Porpoise Library. Her green eyes smiled when she did. Born and raised in New England, she had an uncanny ability to predict the weather. I stopped watching the television reports and called her instead.

"Snow coming?" I'd ask when nature grew still and the winter sky turned thick with clouds.

"Six inches today, clear tomorrow," she might answer.

I HAD TOLD all my friends how sick Sammy was, but none of them had actually seen him because I could not have anyone in the house. When we pulled up at Consolidated that afternoon, it took him a good ten minutes to get out of the van. He finally emerged: hands clawed, back bent, bobbing the top half of his body back and forth as he squinted and grimaced. Just as he stepped out of the van, Carly and her daughter walked out of the school. I saw a look of horror cross Carly's face.

How dare she look at him like that! I was furious to see my own terror reflected in the face of my dear friend, a terror I had successfully kept at bay.

I learned an important lesson that day: no matter how sick the child, no matter how wrenching the situation, a person should always smile at the child's parent.

I held the school door open and waited while Sammy made his tortured way from the van to the building. He jumped and hopped, back and forth, over lines and mats. He held his breath, then gasped for air when he completed a jump. Slowly, painfully, he approached his former teacher, Fern, the one who had told me he had the purest math mind they'd ever seen. I watched with an aching heart as he stood in the center of her room, eyes clenched, hands clawed, trying not to do compulsions. They bantered about mathematics, and we all worked hard to pretend that everything was just like old times. Then the visit ended. He did his best to walk out of the room and into the hall without any compulsions. Fern and I looked quietly at each other.

"God gave him to you for a reason," she said softly.

I bit my lower lip and nodded. Then I followed him down the hall as he struggled out to the van, and we went home.

JAMES WENT OUT for soccer, as he did every year. I always looked forward to soccer season. On Sunday afternoons, four games were played simultaneously across the fields maintained

by the Parks and Recreation Department. I stood on the side-
lines with my friends. We cheered for our kids and caught up
on one another's lives. I always sponsored James's team. They
wore T-shirts plastered with my name and "Law Offices" across
the back. Tracy's son Harrison often played on the same team
as James.

"Shouldn't it just say 'Law Office,' Beth, not 'Offices'?
There's only one of you," Tracy had asked at a game the year
before.

We'd stood in the lush green grass, under a blue sky, on a
brilliant fall afternoon. Her short brown hair glistened with
hints of red.

"No." I smiled back. "There's a bookcase that divides the
space in two, so it's offices—plural." We burst out laughing.

This year, I did not have time for socializing. I brought
James to the field, stuck around for the first ten minutes of each
game, raced home, then went back ten minutes before the end
of the game to watch.

"Why didn't you stay?" James wanted to know.

"I couldn't, love. Sammy's too sick," I said, hurrying him
into the van. Soccer was not fun anymore; it was another obli-
gation.

AS SICK AS SAMMY was, he was determined to keep up with
his work and go to school. The professionals were clear that
going to school would be good for him. I had my doubts but
followed their lead. Because he was not capable of taking the
school bus, I drove him back and forth. It took him over two
hours to complete the compulsions required to leave the house.
He snorted, twitched, and held his breath as he inched his way

to the back door of the house. Finally, he'd make it outside and into the van. Once we arrived at the middle school, I often paced the parking lot while he tried to exit the van. One day, two teachers were conferencing in a first-floor classroom. The window was open, and we spoke through the screen.

"I can't get him out," I said quietly, blinking back tears.

"We know, we've been watching," said Anne, the math team coach. Deep sadness lined her face.

Forty-five minutes later, Sammy and I drove away. He had not been able to leave the van.

SAMMY'S FATHER, WHO WAS still living in California, had a great deal of difficulty accepting Sammy's illness. The children had their own guardian *ad litem* through our divorce proceedings. Together, we called Sammy's dad to explain the seriousness of the situation, but he remained unconvinced and suggested it might be due to overmothering. I asked the guardian *ad litem* to meet with Sammy's teachers and clear up any lingering doubt. Even after that follow-up, Sammy's father was not persuaded.

I WROTE THE PSYCHIATRIST every week to update him on what we called Sammy's progress. In my early letters, I wrote that although we were starting his bedtime routine at six-thirty, it was close to midnight before Sammy was in his bed and asleep. I recorded when he had managed to sit in a chair, or take a shower, or let me brush his teeth. I was excited to report that he had gained six pounds and let us open the windows once in a while. I wrote about when he slept one night in pajamas.

The point of the letters was to track whether the Zoloft was working. Each time Sammy regressed from an improvement, we patiently increased the dose and waited for the signs that meant he was clearly and firmly on the road to recovery. By the third week of September, it seemed that we were headed in the right direction. His body movements were less strained. He twisted and snorted less. For one full week, he made it to school every day. He arrived late, but he was there. He also showered every evening and sat at the table for meals.

I had Devers and a few of Sammy's other friends come to the house one Saturday to play Dungeons & Dragons. I wanted him to remain connected to his peers.

Chris stopped in when she dropped off Devers.

"How's Sammy doing?" she asked, deeply concerned.

"Better, I think," I said, handing her a cup of tea. "He seems to be developing coping strategies. He has such a hard time getting dressed in the morning. Last night he came up with the idea of putting on clean clothes each night before bed, so that he can be ready for school earlier."

"I can't understand it," she said. "He was totally fine last year."

"It's my fault," I admitted quietly. "I shouldn't have bought the house."

"Is that what the doctor says?"

"He says it's some kind of anxiety. What else could it be?" We thoughtfully sipped our tea.

"You've never seen this, in all your work with special needs children?" I asked.

"Never seen it happen like this." She shook her head.

Sammy was able to stay focused while his friends visited.

He loved the intellectual challenge of Dungeons & Dragons, and they tolerated his minor quirks with good humor. Individuals with OCD can sometimes manage their behaviors for defined periods of time, then fall apart later. Sammy kept himself reasonably under control during the game. Once his friends left, he engaged in a storm of compulsions.

I WAS THRILLED BY what I firmly believed were signs of recovery. My late September update to Dr. Drill brimmed with happiness about showers, school days, and eating full meals. I drove Sammy back and forth to school because he was still unable to take the bus, but I knew that would be his next big step.

Then things changed.

First, he missed a day of school. He kept showering and eating, so I thought perhaps it was an isolated incident. But the next week, school was impossible. The twisting and snorting that had faded away now tortured him again. For long periods, he held his T-shirt up to his ears, crossed his eyes while he looked up at the ceiling, and huffed and puffed multiple times in quick succession. He randomly shouted out "Be quiet!" and "Stop it!" He slammed doors five or six times to make sure they were closed. Next he started yelping.

In the language of mental health professionals, he was "decompensating." This meant he was losing his hard-won gains. "Decompensate" is a term like "collateral damage." The word belies the horror. When Sammy decompensated, I walked far into the woods so I could wail from my gut without being overheard by him. When I was done, when I had tapped out all the emotional rage and dried the tears of overbearing sadness, I came back to the house. There I smiled at Sammy, told him how much I loved him, and said that soon he would be better.

"Can I get you anything?" I'd ask desperately as he rubbed his feet back and forth on the rug, his eyes in slits, holding his ears.

Sometimes he'd ask for something; mostly he'd just shake his head no, hold his breath, and gesture for me to leave the room as quickly as possible.

He added a new compulsion, swirling his right foot each time he took a step.

"I've noticed you moving your foot like that," I said and mimicked the swirl with my leg. "Can you explain it to me so that I understand?"

"But, Mom," he said, "that's top secret."

For a few weeks, I clung to the hope that he would turn the corner back to mental health. I carefully followed Dr. Drill's instructions to increase the Zoloft and wait. Dr. Drill was certain Sammy's backslide was due to anxiety and stress. He and Sammy's psychologist felt that with enough time and talk, we would uncover the root cause of his problem. During the short breaks between Sammy's snorts, twists, and other gyrations, I patiently tried to talk with him about what might be causing his anxiety. We reviewed everything—school, home, friends—and came up with nothing.

"I never knew there were so many things to be anxious about," he told me sincerely one day.

Some days, desperate to keep up with school, he would wake and say, "Mom, it's a good day. I think I can go."

I'd look at him, thinking, *There's no way this will work*, but I'd say, "Okay, darling, let's get ready."

He'd begin all the compulsions he needed to do before we left the house: forward and backward steps, twisting and turning while he held his breath, rubbing his feet back and forth, closing his ears with his index fingers and gasping for air, throwing his head back and snapping his neck while he snorted. Two hours later, we'd pull into the school's parking lot. Sometimes he'd make it out of the van and into the building; mostly he wouldn't. He'd cry on the way home. I'd watch him in the rearview mirror, my vision blurred by my tears.

"It's okay, Sammy. We'll try a different day," I'd tell him with a shattered heart.

On one short visit, when he made it into school, he held his shirt up over his head for the entire time. The teacher said that the other students ridiculed him.

At night, he tried to sleep sitting up in his bed. He clicked door locks incessantly. When he showered, he turned the water on and off at least twenty times in succession. His mood alternated between mania and depression. Once, after he spent most of the day at school, he had a complete meltdown: screaming, yelling, virtually hysterical.

As October passed and life became increasingly painful, his will to succeed dwindled. He tried less and less often to go to school. Even taking a few steps into the yard was excruciating for him. He made it to one math meet by sheer force of determination, and there were occasional decent days, but by the middle of November I knew I'd lost my son. Despite all the therapy and medication, Sammy was gone, and the agony was unbearable. I had cried about my marriage, I had cried about my divorce, but nothing compared with the way I cried about my son.

AS THE WEATHER TURNED colder, I had to do something about my kayaks. Snow was coming, and they were tied up at the cove. I called the owner of a boathouse at the end of my old street. He said I could store them there for the winter. Then I called Tracy and set up a time when she could help me put them away. We met one cold morning.

My kayaks are long and sleek and heavy. One by one, we hauled them up the stairs, wedged them through the boat-house door, and then wrestled them to a spot inside. While we struggled, I brought her up to date about Sammy. At last, we had all three kayaks inside.

"I don't think I went kayaking six times this whole sum-mer," I said, patting the last one on its belly as we propped it on its side against one of the walls. I turned to Tracy.

Her dark eyes studied mine.

We reached out and gave each other a quick hug.

"Thanks," I said. "I have to go." Then we locked up the boathouse, and I hurried back to my son.

6

Winter

Winter may begin with a date on the calendar, but as far as I'm concerned, it starts when the first great storm rolls in and dumps a foot or more of snow on Kennebunkport. The day before the storm, everyone goes grocery shopping in case it becomes impossible to leave the house. We complain a bit to one another about the coming storm, but generally everyone is excited.

The truth is, most locals love a good snowstorm, certainly the first one of the year. All the men put their plows on the front of their pickups and stop by Bradbury's for coffee. The plows must be relatively easy to hook up, because I've noticed they are on and off fairly frequently, depending on the weather report.

One time I figured out that two people were dating when I spotted his plow in her driveway.

"Isn't that Bob's plow?" I asked the kids as we drove by Lindy's house.

A few months later, they got married. I've never had a man leave his plow in my driveway, which is perhaps why I'm still single.

On the night before a big storm is due, little kids across the state go to bed with their tiny hearts hoping that "tomorrow will be a snow day." On ordinary school days, experienced mothers might need to clang pots and pans over the heads of their children to wake them. Not when it snows; the kids bound out of bed at the crack of dawn. They race around the house shouting, "Snow day! Snow day!" The parents watch the news, which is temporarily called "Storm Center." The newscasters wear sweaters and hold mugs filled with steaming hot chocolate as they report on the number of inches. A list of school and other closings runs across the bottom of the television screen.

If the big storm hits late in the day, the crews work all night to clear the roads. From my window, I hear the snowplows pass back and forth in the night. I lie in bed, snug as a bug, and listen to them scraping the roads. At daybreak, if the snow is still swirling, it fills my room with blue light the color of robins' eggs. I lie still and try to remember that color, because it is so different from that of any other day. When I get up and look out the window, I can see straight through the woods.

I look forward to the snow because I love to cross-country ski. In less than five minutes, I can pop out my side door, snap on my skis, and be off through the woods. Ten minutes later, I stand on the edge of the marsh, facing the thousands of acres that stretch to the ocean. It is cold and quiet and peaceful. The sun blazes down and reflects brilliantly off the banks of the marsh. The soft rhythm of my skis is mesmerizing as they patiently slide across the snow. It is almost as good as kayaking.

I like to stop and sit on a fieldstone wall. I wonder about the farmer who built it long ago. There are busy days of shoveling and skiing and skating ahead, but for that moment—while the world is quiet and sun graces the tip of my nose—I let the stillness and peace seep into my bones.

Winters were like that for me before Sammy got sick.

THERE WAS SO MUCH snow the first winter Sammy was sick that our plow guy brought in a front-end loader to move it. It piled up around the house and all over the porches. I gazed out the windows, felt the call of the marsh, and knew that I could not leave. In past years, the snow had given me a sense of freedom. This year, it felt like a trap.

"It's snowing, and he's still sick," I sobbed to my mother on the phone when the first snow fell.

It was one of the arbitrary dates I had set for his recovery that never came: Halloween, Thanksgiving, the first snowstorm. Instead of watching him get better, I watched the milligrams on his prescription rise. He had started at .25 milligrams of Zoloft. He was up to 137.5 milligrams, and still there was no improvement. In fact, he was worse.

There were still days when he insisted on trying to go to school. If he made it into the building, he could not touch the two-foot band of blue carpet that bordered the halls holding the lockers. The only way he could open his locker—and he insisted on keeping his books there, like everyone else—was to stand with his feet outside the blue band and throw his body at the locker. With his body angled, feet outside the blue band, shoulder resting on the metal casing, he opened his locker and retrieved his books. Then he would slam his locker shut and push himself off and into a standing position. Next he had to get to the classroom. Once he worked up the courage to touch the doorknob—holding his breath, swirling his leg, squinting and blinking his eyes—he would fling open the classroom door and leap in over the blue band.

"Sammy!" His geography teacher exclaimed with welcome and excitement as the door flew open.

I waited in the hall and watched until he was safely in the classroom.

One day, a sixth-grade girl went to her locker just in time to watch him leap into the classroom. She came up to me.

"Are you Sammy's mother?"

"Yes." I was afraid of what I might hear next.

"I think he is so cool." She smiled and beamed up at me.

"I do, too." I smiled back, noticing the golden light that suddenly glistened all around her.

AT OUR NEXT SESSION, the psychologist asked me to find out what behavior was causing Sammy the most anxiety at school. The plan was to tackle one behavior at a time. When Sammy had mastered one behavior, they would move on to conquer the next. The technique is called Exposure Response Prevention, or ERP. In our house, we called it "urp."

I dutifully e-mailed his homeroom teacher and asked the question. She wrote back, "I think the behavior that stands out the most is jumping over the blue part of the rug while entering classrooms or flinging himself at the lockers, and the way he goes to classes/lunch while walking down the hall (climbing under and over something imaginary near the lighted section by the bathroom) and the way he follows a pattern while kind of running in spurts down the hall, holding his breath, bent over in the shape of an upside-down L."

Where exactly, I wondered, would one start?

By virtue of sheer determination, Sammy still made it to every math meet. Meets were held at the Portland Exposition Building, a huge hall that hosts trade events like car shows and boat extravaganzas. For math meets, the Expo was set up like a giant classroom. Hundreds of tables were placed in rows across the floor, each with six folding chairs and a sign for a school. The tables were grouped by grade level. At the front of the hall was a microphone for the chair of the Southern Maine Math League. Over the entrance hung an electronic clock with a buzzer.

It was an excruciating process to get Sammy into the Expo for the meets; there were so many lines and mats and patterns to cross from the street, through the lobby, and into the hall. But once he was inside and seated, he was still—almost—at the top of his game. He was so proud of his skill in mathematics. He was devastated the one time he had to go to a meet as a team alternate because he had not been able to make the practices. As an alternate, he took the same test as the team members and his scores were tallied, but they did not count for the competition. When the results came back, he had outscored every member of the team. The team did not place at that meet.

"Even if he can't make the practices," the math team coach told me afterward, "from now on, he's on the team."

At home, he became incapable of doing almost anything for himself. He spent all day downstairs in the den and came upstairs only for bed at night. There were so many compulsions involved in getting from one floor to the next that one trip up and down the stairs was all he could handle in a day. He inexplicably stuck his head in a cabinet when he traveled between the first and second floors.

He stopped flushing the toilet entirely. He yelped all night while he slept.

Sleep, for me, was a memory. Sometimes I never made it to my room. I lugged my dead-tired body over to the couch on the second floor and collapsed after a full day of watching compulsions and racking my brain over every aspect of our lives to detect anxiety. I constantly wondered if I might have caused this disorder: the divorce, the move, my need for a clean kitchen. There had to be something.

Along the way, I'd do a little work, sell off investments to pay the bills, administer medication, get Sammy what he needed, drive him back and forth for a half day/few hours/ another failed attempt at school, fix meals, do laundry, drive James where he needed to go, help him with his homework, finally get both boys into their rooms for the night, and then head for the couch. A few hours after collapsing on the couch, I'd wake and drag myself up the stairs to my room. I'd fall into bed and then wake periodically all night long. Sometimes I woke when I heard Sammy yelp. Sometimes I woke when I heard a thud. Sometimes I just woke.

What was that? would suddenly rush through my sleeping brain, flooding me with adrenaline and jolting me wide-awake.

I'd lie there, listening and wondering if I needed to get up and check on him. Most times I hauled my weary self downstairs and listened quietly outside his door. If I was certain he was asleep, that it had been a false alarm, I'd pull myself back upstairs to bed. Eventually, I would fall into what passed for sleep again, only to startle awake within an hour or two.

On the other hand, if I heard yelping or pounding or rubbing of feet, I'd lie down on the floor outside his closed door. I'd wait until the sounds subsided and I knew he was sleeping again. Calling his name to ask if he needed me only made it worse. He was devastated that I was aware of his nighttime behaviors. He felt guilty about hurting me with his pain. So I kept my quiet vigil on the other side of the door.

Mental illness, like any other serious disease, affects the whole family, and we all became slaves to the disorder. When James was home, he became a mini version of me, catering to Sammy's needs. When Sammy bellowed my name for the hundredth time, James might say, "I'll go, Mom." I was too weary to protest, but it hurt to see my eight-year-old burdened.

Midway through the winter, the boys started fighting like cats and dogs.

"Stop that right now," I shouted one afternoon as I bounded into the den. Sammy, who was holding a book, threw it at me. I pivoted, and it whizzed by my ear.

James was sobbing. Sammy burst into tears.

"What is going on here?"

"It's Sammy!" cried James. "He's taking the thing I love the most and using it against me."

"James!" Sammy screamed.

"One at a time! One at a time. C'mon now, quiet down. You'll each tell me your side of it. No interruptions or comments while the other person talks, and you'll each have as many turns as you need." I sat down on the couch, and I listened.

"Sammy won't play with me unless I do what he wants. He always says, 'James, I'll do role-playing games if you'll open the door' or 'if you'll get me Kleenex.' It's not fair, and I have to keep doing it. I wish I hated playing with him; but I want to do role-playing so much that I'll do whatever he wants. And it's not fair. He should just play with me!" James started sobbing again.

"But—" began Sammy.

"Not yet, Sammy. We'll wait for James to finish." I turned back to James. "You let us know when you're done with your side."

He sniffled and nodded. "I'm done."

Sammy stood at the side of the room, bent over, and rubbed his feet.

"I give and give and give, but it's never enough for him. I can't do any better than I'm doing!" he screamed through his own sobs.

My heart broke for both of them.

"Okay, let's have a rule," I said quietly. "No more bribes. If Sammy needs help, he asks for it. If James does not want to do it, he calls me and I come. No more throwing things, either. Okay?"

Both boys agreed.

After that, I tried to keep James out of the house as much as possible. I enrolled him in a stream of after-school programs: arts and crafts, cooking, computer class, whatever was offered.

"I want to come home after school," James whined one day as he watched me filling out another form.

"No, you don't." I signed the form and sealed the envelope.

IN THE EMPTY HOUSE, Sammy and I worked on pinpointing his anxiety by completing anxiety thermometers. They were labeled from zero to ten. Zero was anxiety-free, at the bottom of the thermometer. It had a happy face with lots of z's surrounding it to represent sleep. I had some doubts about sleep being anxiety-free because Sammy was yelping and scratching in his sleep, but compared to what went on when he was awake, it made sense. As the faces climbed the number scale, they escalated in anxiety. The number ten face showed a scream with tears coming out of its eyes. Sammy put "School" toward the bottom with a borderline happy face. "Reading" was next to face number five, which had a relatively flat expression. Reading had always been tough for him, so that made sense. He was not able to assign any labels next to faces six through ten, so we still had no clue as to what was causing all the anxiety.

JOSH WAS HOME from boarding school only periodically. Every time he came back, he was taller. He was lucky to be away. He did not know how truly desperate our lives had become. In the middle of December, he came home for a month. On the ride home from the bus stop, I brought him up to date on all the latest information about Sammy's condition.

"I think he's doing better," I concluded. Maybe if I said it enough, it would be true.

The next morning, I fixed breakfast for Josh.

"Sammy's doing better, don't you think?" I asked, sliding the scrambled eggs from the pan to his plate.

"No, Mom, he's not," Josh answered impatiently. "And why do you keep saying he's getting better when he's not?"

A muffin popped up from the toaster. I grabbed it and dropped it on the plate.

"Because if I thought this was it, that he'd never get better, and that for the rest of our lives it would be like this, I'm not sure I could get up in the morning and keep going." I shoved the plate at him. "Got it?"

Josh nodded yes.

BY NEW YEAR'S, I had decided to keep Sammy home entirely. There was no payoff to the agonizing attempts and failures associated with school. Maybe if he stayed home it would give him the time and space he needed to let things settle down. I reasoned that he could make a fresh start when everyone went back after the February break. Perhaps by then we would have discovered and overcome the anxiety that propelled his disorder. We completed time lines with our family history, searching to find the root of the problem. I began speaking with the school staff to find out if we could design an individualized program for him.

Keeping Sammy home gave my life a semblance of regularity for the first time in months. I was no longer consumed by trying to get him back and forth to school. I was no longer on pins and needles waiting for the inevitable telephone call about him having a meltdown, and my needing to go get him right away.

It seemed to be helping him, too. He was doing less jumping, hopping, and leg swirling, and he was flushing the toilet on a regular basis. He was eating and sleeping well. He ventured outside sometimes. I bit my tongue because although it was so cold, he would not wear a coat. I knew that if I insisted on a jacket, he'd choose to remain a prisoner in the house rather than tackle the overwhelming task of getting himself into and out of another garment. Instead, I tried to be outside when he was, in order to monitor whether he was too cold. I pretended to shovel or clean out the car or do some other menial task, so that he did not know I was keeping an eye on him.

One day, he tried to help me shovel the snow and suddenly starting crying.

"Oh, darling, what is it?" I asked, wanting so badly to be able to wrap him in my arms but knowing that touching him would set off a round of compulsions.

"Why did you have to get divorced? Why couldn't we be like everyone else?"

"I wish it hadn't happened, and it's sad that it didn't work out." I wiped the drips from my leaky eyes, wishing I could wipe his instead. "But I'd never take back a minute of my life, because I have the three of you."

"I just wish we could be normal!" he cried.

"Sammy, lots of kids think their families aren't normal. Devers told his mom that he wishes his family were normal, and his parents are married."

He shoveled a little more, then stopped.

"On the *Today* show, they said lots of parents are divorced. Maybe we are normal," he said through softening tears.

"Or maybe there's no such thing as normal," I added.

He smiled. I felt good. *Maybe that's it,* I thought. *Maybe that's been the problem all along, and now that he's accepted the di-vorce, his anxiety will fade and he'll get better.*

Wishful thinking.

AS WITH SLEEP, sitting in a chair was only a fond memory for me. There was always something else to be done. I was constantly running up and down stairs to get him things or open doors or help him with one of a thousand tasks.

I called my mom. "Am I enabling him?" I wondered.

"You have to help him, Beth, he's just too sick," she answered.

I would be up in my third-floor office, attempting to work, when he'd bellow for me from the first-floor den. I'd charge down the two flights to see what he needed. When his voice was particularly frantic, I'd know he needed me to open a door right away. Since he avoided bathrooms as much as possible, it was easier for him to walk into the woods to relieve himself. He could not, however, open the door to get outside. He also waited until the very last minute to call me. I'd race downstairs and into the den.

"Mom, I want to go outside for a walk!" He'd be hopping from one foot to the other, like a little boy who suddenly had to go.

I'd rush to open the door, knowing full well he'd explode if I didn't hurry. He'd run outside in his contorted way. I'd leave the door open and go back up to my third-floor office. I waited up there because he got uptight about inconveniencing me if I stayed downstairs. Ten or so minutes later, I'd hear him calling me, and I'd know he was back inside. I'd go downstairs to close the door. Then he'd ask me for something to eat. I'd go upstairs and bring it back down, then I'd climb the two flights back to my office. Twenty minutes later, the whole thing would start over.

James had a set of walkie-talkies. We put one downstairs in the den and the other in my office. This made it easier for Sammy to reach me quickly.

"What would happen in a fire?" I asked Sammy one day. "How would you get out?" I watched him rubbing his feet back and forth, repeating the few steps he'd just taken into the den.

"If there's an emergency, it's different," he answered confidently, with barely a break in his motions.

"So you could open a door and get out?" I needed to know if I could ever leave the house again. Maybe I needed to ask my friends to do my grocery shopping.

"Yes," he answered quickly, nodding, intent on his compulsions.

I STILL HAD NOT told Sammy the name of his disorder. There are two theories when it comes to children and mental illness. One is to treat the behaviors and keep the diagnosis confidential. The other is to share the diagnosis. Even some grown-ups never fully recover from some truths, so when it comes to children, I feel it is best to err on the side of caution.

Another reason to be cautious is that a mental illness diagnosis is never certain, and once a child is labeled, it tends to stick. Unlike cancer or diabetes or HIV, there is no test that can pinpoint a brain disorder. Instead, there are a series of diagnostic criteria that lend themselves to a diagnosis "consistent with" a particular disorder. Sammy's behaviors were "consistent with" a diagnosis of obsessive-compulsive disorder.

As time went on, I had to admit that his behaviors did indeed appear consistent with OCD. He was inexplicably driven to follow a set of rules that forced him to endlessly repeat certain behaviors. What I found troubling, though, was that the OCD had come out of nowhere and hit him like a sledgehammer. The diagnosis just didn't feel right. Dr. Drill essentially said, "It happens," but I relentlessly scoured the Internet for an explanation. I didn't find one.

Months earlier, my sister Sue had mentioned that there was research showing a possible link between OCD and strep infections. I found the research on the National Institute of Mental Health's Web site. I was relatively sure that Sammy had never had a strep throat, and in any case, the research was confined to much younger children. Nonetheless, I had his pediatric records searched back to birth. The search confirmed my recollection: no strep. As I surrendered myself to the fact that my son might have a lifelong brain disorder, I began to believe that information might be his best tool.

When *Time* devoted an entire issue to mental health, it gave me an opening.

"*Time* magazine has an interesting article this week," I mentioned as I watched him rub his feet back and forth on the carpet. "It says there are different types of serotonin issues. Some people get depressed, but other people have to do things over and over. It's called obsessive-compulsive disorder."

"Mr. Hill's brother had excessive-compulsive disorder," Sammy puffed out between rubs. Mr. Hill was his fifth-grade teacher. "I've probably got it, too, except I can stop whenever I want," he added.

"Then why do you do it?" I asked.

"Because it makes life more interesting." He held his ears shut with his fingertips while he said this.

"That's great, sweetheart." I watched him duck and high-step over the opening to a hallway, as if there were an imaginary pole there; then he held his breath and hopped away.

THE SCHOOL PERSONNEL AGREED that they could no longer educate Sammy within the building's four walls. We set up an individualized program that included working with his former reading teacher at Consolidated. I would take him once a week. A second tutor would come to the house to work with him when he was able.

For about six weeks, things went relatively well. Then there was a shift. I could tell when Sammy was going to decompensate. It was not that the compulsions themselves changed; it was their level of intensity and frequency. He always huffed and puffed. The change was when he huffed and puffed in rapid succession, gasped for breath, broke out in a sweat, rubbed his feet back and forth, waved me out of the room, held his ears shut, and was unable to talk, all at the same time. When his compulsions engulfed every last bit of his energy and concentration, I knew he would soon implode.

So it was with hesitation that I dropped Sammy at Consolidated one afternoon to work with his reading tutor. He insisted he was well enough to go, but I knew better. He was close to falling apart. How could I say that to him? He wanted so badly to succeed. He jerked, hopped, and swirled his way down the hall to the reading teacher's room. I rushed off to the grocery store. I expected the call to come, and it did. The cell phone rang as I was loading the groceries into the back of the van.

"Beth, you have to come right away." The teacher's voice was urgent and scared. "I can't get him out of the bathroom, and he won't talk to me."

"Tell him I'm coming. I'm at the grocery store, but I'll leave right now." I threw the last two bags into the back of the van and took off.

By the time I pulled up, he was standing at the school door. He ran out to the van, his back humped. The teacher followed behind him. I slid the van door open. Sammy climbed in, and I slid the door closed. The van doors were among the things he no longer touched.

"He is a completely different child than I have ever seen before," the teacher said as she gave me a small piece of paper. "He wouldn't talk to me, wouldn't spell his words; he wouldn't even look at me. He just wrote this and handed it to me."

I unfolded the paper and looked down.

Sammy had printed the word "HELP."

7

Spring

Spring frequently skips past Maine. While the rest of the country is planting, we are often continuing our relationships with the men who plow. It's one of those liaisons a single woman really wants to end, but—thank goodness—the man keeps coming back.

So while others are out there sowing their seeds, we're still shoveling and salting and hoping for change. Yet when the snow is almost gone and winter's over, I always feel a touch sad and regretful, as if something special has been lost that might not come again. Then, in a blink, the birds are back and everything changes.

"Did you hear the peepers?" we ask one another excitedly about the frogs.

The males call for mates from every pond, almost round the clock. I crack my window open, so that I can fall asleep to their song. It starts as a low, throaty squawk but soon sounds like a million chirping crickets. After a month or so, they're gone. The foghorn blares from the lighthouse, warmer days come in waves, and friends begin to talk about their gardens.

I do not join in because I do not garden. I have killed almost every plant I have ever tried to grow.

My friend Marty said, "You're not using the right materials."

She sat at a card table in Bradbury's parking lot on a gray morning. Large plastic bags of fertilizer were piled up around the table. Big black-and-white cows' heads were stamped onto each bag. She was part of a mothers' group that was fundraising by selling the fertilizer.

"Try some of this." She slapped one of the cows across the muzzle. "Good day to get started."

I looked at the sky and stated the obvious: "It's dreary and gray."

"Not this afternoon—sunny and beautiful."

I knew better than to disagree with her about the weather.

"The problem isn't the materials," I said. "At a certain point, a person accepts their limitations. Gardening is off the list. I'll give you a donation, though." I reached in my pocket for a few dollars.

"Been kayaking yet?" she asked, taking the money.

"Not yet."

Sammy was too ill for me to leave him that spring.

JAMES AND I stood at the end of our road, waiting for his school bus. It was April and warming up, but we were still in ski jackets, with rubber boots on our feet.

"Why are you crying, Mom?" James asked in his sweet third grader's voice.

"Because the snow is melting" leaked out through my tears. "I thought he'd be well by the time the snow melted. He's been sick for a very long time, and I guess he's not going to get better."

James was quiet for a thoughtful moment. "I don't remember what Sammy was like before." His ocean eyes, lit with traces of tears, looked up at me.

"He was like you, love," I answered, wiping his tears away.

Despite all the psychological counseling, psychiatric appointments, and medication, Sammy had ended the winter in much worse shape than he had started it. He now had verbal tics that peppered his speech like hiccups. At first, they came occasionally, with the same sudden jump that lands in the middle of a boy's words when puberty is in the offing. I thought perhaps his voice was changing. As time went on, though, there were more and more tics, with no change in Sammy's pitch. In the beginning, he suffered through them as an annoyance. Within a few weeks, they had completely changed his speech pattern.

IN FEBRUARY, I FOUND research stating that tics might be seasonal, so I cashed in my frequent-flier miles and took us to Florida for a week, thinking maybe the warmth would help.

Getting Sammy to and from the plane was challenging, but he managed with the same brave determination that got him to math meets. It took him a day to get over the plane ride, but then he did well. During the day, he collected pieces of broken coral that had washed up on the shore. He swam in the pool. We went out for pizza. At night, he stayed on the couch in my room. It was not until we shared a room that I realized the verbal tics also streamed out all night long.

He felt so much better when we got back home that he wanted to try school again.

"Great!" I gulped, trying to sound optimistic.

He had seemed to stabilize within the framework of being incredibly ill, and I was wary that school might trigger a regression. I was also worried about how his classmates would treat him. He looked overgrown and unkempt. He rarely bathed, wore the same clothes for days, and would not put on a pair of socks. His sense of touch was so heightened that cutting his hair caused him pain, so it hung in long, greasy clumps.

After a couple of discussions, the school administrators said they thought he would do well in a room for students with special needs. They said he would have maximum flexibility there, and that he could also spend time in his regular classroom. Sammy and I were excited. We called it the "too-good-to-be-true room."

When I dropped Sammy off that first morning, he went directly to his beloved math. From there, he went to the too-good-to-be-true room. The too-good-to-be-true class went to do some cooking. He did an excellent job of cutting summer squash. He held himself together even though he later told me that the pattern on the floor made him "uncomfortable." After lunch, they went back to the too-good-to-be-true room for journaling, and that's when it all fell apart.

Journaling, I learned later, followed after the teacher read a fact out loud from *The Guinness Book of Records*. The class talked about the item for a while; then the teacher wrote a sentence about it on the board. The class was expected to add the correct capitalization and punctuation to the sentence. After that, she had them all "journal" about what they had learned.

Partway through this journaling, Sammy was bored out of his skull.

"I'm ready to go," he announced to the teacher.

She told him he couldn't leave.

"Under the plan, I can go," he said.

"That's not part of the plan." She refused to let him leave.

"Then I quit the plan!" Sammy burst into tears.

"You can't quit," said the teacher.

"Oh, yes, I can! I quit!"

They went back and forth for a while: no you can't, yes I can. Then she gave him three choices. He could stay in her room, go to the social worker's office, or go to Mr. Perrin's room.

"I'll go see Mr. Perrin!" Sammy bolted. He did not know Mr. Perrin, so he went directly to the office and said he needed to use the phone to call his mother. By this point, he was extremely anxious and frantic.

The secretary there told him that to use the telephone he had to get permission from the vice principal, who turned out to be Mr. Perrin. Sammy urgently told Mr. Perrin that he needed to call me. Mr. Perrin had no familiarity with the situation and wanted an explanation of what had happened. Making Sammy retell the story frustrated him even more.

Finally, Sammy gave up and made a grab for the telephone. They ended up in a physical struggle. Mr. Perrin, a burly Brian Dennehy type, won. Then the too-good-to-be-true teacher showed up and went through the entire story again. She said that for Sammy to leave her class, they would have to re-arrange the entire school system to accommodate one student, which they would not do.

"WELL, THEN! YOU DON'T KNOW MY MOTHER!" Sammy screamed.

When they finally called me, I could hear him yelling in the background. I was steaming when I arrived at the school, but I kept my thoughts to myself, retrieved my son, and left. The principal called later to apologize.

"These things happen," I told her. We set another meeting to figure out what had gone wrong.

In spite of my having confirmed twice in advance that Sammy could come and go from the too-good-to-be-true room, I was told at the meeting that my understanding was not accurate. The teacher attributed the confusion to "a bad choice of words." This was the first piece of information that caused me to pause. There had been no confusion or bad choice of words in our discussion. My job as a lawyer is to get it right.

The second piece that concerned me was the teacher's reaction when the school social worker reported a conversation he'd had with Sammy. Sammy had spoken with the social worker just before cutting summer squash. He had described his own ideas for an economic recovery plan for the country, as well as his feelings about hydrogen-powered cars and their impact on the environment. The social worker relayed this at our meeting, praising the depth of consideration that Sammy had given the problems, as well as his grasp of the issues. When the social worker finished, the too-good-to-be-true teacher piped up.

"It's all fine and good to talk about economic recovery plans and hydrogen-powered cars, but we have a curriculum," she said.

It was right then that I announced that I had thought things over and decided that Sammy would not be returning to her classroom.

Two weeks later I was back at school for another meeting. This time I brought Sammy with me. Gathered at the conference room table, in addition to Sammy and me, were the middle school principal, the math team coach, the school's social worker, the school district's director of special education, Sammy's homeroom teacher, and the district's psychologist. At my request, the too-good-to-be-true teacher had not been invited. Sammy sat at the end of the table in his rumpled clothes, with his dirty hair and eyes like slits, twitching as he spoke with his tic-riddled voice. He told them that he knew they were all trying to help him, but that he just wanted to go back to his regular classes for two days a week. He sat still for as long as he could; then he had to get up and move around. He could not stop his body from jerking.

I was very proud of my son and how he handled that meeting.

We left with a new plan in place. He would start going to school on Tuesdays and Fridays. On Mondays and Thursdays, he would be tutored at home. On Wednesdays, he would rest.

After the meeting, I waited and watched in the middle school lobby while Sammy clung to the wall by the water fountain. One leg was bent and lifted off the floor. He was catching his breath and plotting the route he'd hop to reach the front door. Max, a former classmate from Consolidated, approached him.

"Here, Sammy." Max reached into his pocket and pulled out a Hershey's chocolate kiss.

Sammy moved one hand from the wall and, balancing like a stork, took the chocolate.

"Thanks!" He smiled and popped it into his pocket.

On the way home in the van, Sammy carefully peeled the foil off the candy and ate it.

"Wasn't that nice of him, Mom?"

"Yes, that was very nice."

TWO WEEKS LATER was the third math meet of the year. At the Expo, Sammy hopped over crosswalks and into the building's lobby, where he twitched and jerked and bounced around in circles. He jumped patterns on the floor while he tried to figure out how to get himself out of the lobby and into the giant hall. Every so often, he stopped and glanced up at the beckoning hall that was set up and ready for the competition; then he started hopping again. Finally, he inched his way through the lobby along the sides of mud mats, being careful not to let his feet touch them. At the doorway, he ducked, leapt, and raced into the main hall. It had taken over twenty minutes, but he'd made it.

In the final round of the team competition, with twenty-two seconds to go, a loud disagreement broke out at Sammy's sixth-grade table. The kids were stuck and couldn't agree on how to solve the last problem. One of the boys slammed his fist on the table while two of the girls fervently shook their heads no.

"Wait!" Sammy jumped out of his seat. "That's not it. Watch!"

Sammy scratched equations furiously across a clean sheet of paper.

"But what about this . . ." A boy with dark, curly hair scratched different numbers and symbols onto another sheet of paper.

"No, Sammy's right!" Devers shouted. He grabbed Sammy's scratch work. He slowly followed the line of pencil marks across with his index finger, then stabbed at a number. "Look—right there."

They all huddled and looked.

A girl with chestnut hair slapped herself on the forehead. "He's right. Quick! We'll change it." She snapped up the answer sheet and erased.

"Hurry!" they all urged.

She marked in the new answer just as the buzzer sounded. Exhausted, they collapsed in their seats. Twenty minutes later, the results were announced. Sammy had won second place in the individual competition.

For turning in a perfect paper, the team had won first place in the Southern Maine Math League.

ONE OF THE THINGS about being a lawyer is that your friends will sometimes have legal problems and need your advice. Sometimes their friends will have troubles, too. So when my friend Marty called with a request to meet a friend of hers who was going through a divorce, I said, "Could you just have him call me?"

"I thought you two might get along," Marty answered.

It took a minute for this to register.

"You mean a *date*?" I asked this so sharply that I frightened even myself.

"Well, coffee," she said.

"Marty, I can't even go kayaking. You really think I'm going to leave Sammy to have coffee with a guy I've never met?"

"I could watch Sammy," she offered.

"Nah."

"There's no time you'd be willing to go?" she asked.

"Well, let me think about this. . . . Maybe sometime if Josh was home and things were good with Sammy, I could call this guy, if my hair was clean, and see if he'd meet me in five minutes. As long as he didn't mind my leaving if my pager went off. Think he'd go for that?"

There was an uncomfortable silence.

"So—no men, huh?" Marty asked.

"Not unless he's a child psychiatrist."

We hung up.

BY THE END OF April, Sammy was once again randomly in and out of school, unable to maintain a schedule. In addition to all of the old compulsions, he'd added a few new ones. He sat in his chair at the kitchen table, with his eyes closed and lips pursed, and spurted trumpet noises in rapid succession. Just when James and I relaxed a bit, believing it had stopped, he would start up again. We felt like we were under rapid-fire assault, lacking only the bullets.

Next, he added a phrase that he recited in quick, rhythmic succession: "nothing-is-nothing-is-nothing-is-nothing-is-nothing" . . . *pause* . . . "nothing-is-nothing-is-nothing-is-nothing-is-nothing" . . . *pause* . . . "nothing-is-nothing-is-nothing-is-nothing-is-nothing." Bursts of trumpet fire occasionally interrupted the repetitions.

"Honey, please don't do that," I'd say. He'd stare at me with a blank face and keep going.

"You have to stop that, Sammy. It's really annoying," I said impatiently when the unrelenting noises had continued for over an hour. But he couldn't stop.

"Stop it. Stop it right now!" I shouted when I couldn't take it anymore. He stared right at me, his face void of emotion, and kept making the noises. He could not control himself. I felt like a heel for losing my temper, but I quickly forgave myself, recognizing that at this moment it was more than I could bear.

I called Dr. Drill. "This isn't OCD," I told him. "It's something else."

Sammy started doing something new in the bathroom. I listened outside the door and could tell from the sounds that it had something to do with the drawers in the bathroom cabinet. I suspected he was using the drawers as steps.

He stopped flushing the toilet again and resumed permanent residence on the couch in the den. When he occasionally changed his clothes, it took him forty-five minutes to do so.

He told me the house was full of invisible walls. They sprouted like lasers in every direction, from electrical outlets, television sets, portable telephones, and DVD players. The beams formed a complicated series of barriers. He had to step over or duck under each one, depending on their location. They accounted for the Spider-Man-like way he made his way through the house. He clung to the actual walls or, when he let go, moved like a thief after a protected gem.

We taped up all the openings from which the invisible walls might pop, but they managed to sneak through the tape. Even when the invisible walls were missing, he still had to go under and over where they might be. If he touched one by accident, he had to start the process all over again. Since the walls were invisible, he could never be sure whether he had touched them, so he went through the motions again and again.

EACH MORNING HE HAD to have a series of different drinks.

"Mom, I'll take the usual" was his coded request.

I lined them up on the counter: milk, orange juice, apple juice, pink lemonade, and grape juice. He wanted just an inch or so of each, but he could not start his day without those five drinks. He seemed to have a particular order in which he had to drink them, but I was not able to figure it out. I experimented by putting them in different colored cups on the counter and by pouring them to different levels in the cups. None of that seemed to matter. It was only important that he have all of them, every morning, before he did anything else.

He told me he had psychic powers.

He stopped walking entirely. He jumped and hopped instead. The pounding, pounding, pounding was relentless. Lamps fell off tables. Smoke detectors fell off the walls. When he moved around on the second floor, he jumped so high that I thought he might knock himself out on the open staircase that led to my loft.

"Please, Sammy . . . your head!"

He ignored me and concentrated on his newest compulsion, a complex movement that involved grunting, holding his breath, pressing his ears shut, and then jumping—over and over and over again.

The school called me in again. They wanted Sammy to walk, not hop, when he made his rare appearances.

"He can't," I said, shrugging my shoulders.

Second was the issue of where he hopped off to sometimes. One day, he went missing. When two teachers and the social worker couldn't find him, they went into a panic, until they realized that he couldn't hop far. They doubled back and found him in the library.

"Threaten him with the too-good-to-be-true room if he hops off course again," I suggested. "Or maybe something about insurance claims and knee injuries"—I shrugged again—"might work."

The third issue was unrelated to the hopping. He had told his math team coach that when he ran into a tough problem, he consulted his friend "Joe from China." He'd also consulted Joe once during a tutoring session. He and Joe always reached the right answer, but the teachers were rightfully concerned that he was hallucinating.

I wrote Dr. Drill about this: "I really do not think he is hallucinating. I do not ever see him having conversations with an imaginary person, but I thought I should mention this. Especially since maybe I'm in denial, which would probably be appropriate at this point."

Next, Sammy started locking himself in the bathroom for two or three hours at a time. He screamed and howled in

agony. I lay curled on the floor outside the door with an unbearable pain in my own gut.

My mother called. "There's a medicine called Tenex," she
said. "I read that it helps with tics."

It was about then that Dr. Drill and I began to discuss
whether Sammy's behaviors might be "consistent with"
Tourette syndrome. Dr. Drill said that almost everyone with
Tourette's has symptoms of OCD, although the reverse is not
true. Perhaps it wasn't a serotonin issue after all. Maybe the
problem was a different brain chemical: dopamine.

"Tourette's?" I wondered. "How on earth can he have
Tourette's?"

There was simply no family history of Tourette's anywhere
to be found. I could extrapolate my need for an organized
desk and a clean kitchen to signs that OCD was embedded in
my genetic code. Symptoms of Tourette's, however, were
nonexistent on either side of the family. The one positive
thing that this possible diagnosis did was to absolve me of any
and all guilt. I was willing to accept responsibility for almost
anything. This one, however, was out of the question, and I
stopped beating myself up for the move. Home ownership
could not be responsible for Tourette's. I knew it couldn't be
responsible for OCD, either, but this finally flipped the switch
on my needless guilt.

I researched Tourette's online for hours. I ordered books
about it from Amazon.com. I collected used textbooks from
my friends who were psychology majors. The more I read, the
more convinced I became. He had 90 percent of the symptoms they described.

A week later, Sammy scratched himself until he bled.

"We have to do something. He's hurting himself!" I told Dr. Drill. "If he's got it, we need to treat it."

Dr. Drill increased the Zoloft from 137.5 milligrams to 150. Within a few weeks, he said, we would be adding another medication: clonidine or maybe risperidone. Sammy had me call Dr. Drill back a day or two after the increase. He wanted to know whether the Zoloft itself might be causing the behaviors. Dr. Drill said it could happen, but he did not think this was Sammy's situation.

Once again, we waited and hoped for the increased dose to kick in. In the meantime, I researched clonidine and risperidone. The literature was consistent in suggesting that clonidine was the best way to go, if it worked. Dr. Drill called the prescription into Colonial. The final math meet of the year was coming up shortly. We decided to wait until after the meet to start the clonidine.

8

Colony Beach

Kennebunkport starts to stir as the weather warms up. Cy-clists return to the roads. Geese return from the south. I return to my kayak. I am not out there consistently, but here and there when the sun shines and the water is smooth. I wear a wet suit and stay in the cove. I do not venture into the ocean because the water is frigid. Each spring, boaters die along the coast of Maine. It's often because they are not wearing a life vest. I always wear mine.

As I paddle, I watch the trees come to life, and my muscles grow stronger with every pull. The island trees start first. They are the last to change color in October, and the first to bud in May. A few weeks after the buds, the coastline explodes in green. Wildlife takes over the marsh. Birds nest in the grass. Gulls swoop overhead. Deer gallop past me along the side of the creek. Sometimes the beauty is so overwhelming that I have to stop, hold my boat still, and let it all soak in.

The swell of the water, the push of the breeze, the sheer scope of the ocean: nothing restores me like kayaking.

Sammy turned thirteen on May 17. He had been sick for almost a year, and my boats were still in the boathouse.

BY THE DAY of the final math meet, thirty seconds did not pass without Sammy having a tic or compulsion. I drove him to the Expo. It took him about half an hour to get into the lobby, where he twitched, jerked, and hopped around in circles for another twenty minutes before leaping into the giant hall. He made his way slowly down the rows of competitors and sat at his team's table.

He jerked and snorted, he huffed and puffed; but when the test was placed in front of him, the compulsions stopped and he gave it his complete concentration. He did well on the arithmetic portion, but the geometry (which he had never studied) was difficult for him. Sammy did not place in the individual competition, but the team placed third.

"Mom, I want to ride with the team," he told me, buoyed by the win. "And then take the bus home."

"Sammy . . . ," I began, heartbroken for him.

He wanted so badly to be like all the other kids in sixth grade.

"Mom, please . . . I can do it!"

"I don't think . . ."

"Please, Mom. I can do it."

"You'll have to get off this bus in front of the school, walk all the way through the school, and then go out the back door to catch the bus home." Perhaps I could reason with him. "There won't be enough time. Maybe a different day—"

"I can do it!" he shouted.

I sighed and relented.

"All right. I'll be home when you get there."

The bus pulled away from the Expo, and I headed for the courthouse, just five minutes away. There was a short meeting scheduled in a judge's chambers. By this point, I was attending most meetings by telephone. The chance to show up for a meeting in person was too good an opportunity to miss.

My pager went off just as I was leaving the judge's chambers. I recognized the phone number. It was the middle school. I raced out of the courthouse and dialed my cell phone while I ran to the parking garage.

Sammy sobbed and screamed in the background, while the math team coach told me what had happened.

After multiple excruciating attempts to exit the bus, he had finally made it off. Then he'd spotted lines in a crosswalk that needed jumping. Hunched over, he'd doubled back in front of the bus to reach the crosswalk. The driver, not anticipating that any of the students would duck in front of the bus, almost ran him over.

"For the longest time, we couldn't get him off the crosswalk," the coach continued. "He just kept jumping the lines. When he finally started toward the building, he kept hopping around on the bricks in front of the door. I couldn't get him to stop. Finally, I went and got his homeroom teacher. She came out, took one look, and said, 'It's not going to happen. Just call his mother and she'll come get him.' He's screaming because he thinks we made him miss the bus."

"Okay, let me talk to him."

"Sammy, your mom wants to talk to you."

He came on the line, sobbing. "I could have done it, Mom. They wouldn't let me!"

"I know, honey. You just needed more time. I'm coming for you. It's okay."

I roared out of Portland and onto the turnpike. Once he was relatively stable, I hung up and began sobbing myself. I called my mother while I drove.

"I can't do it anymore! I've tried everything, and I can't help him. James is suffering. I'm on the verge of collapse. I've got three kids, and I can't even earn a living." I gulped for air. "He takes everything I've got, and I'm not helping him get better! I've got nothing left to give and nothing else to try. It's depressing to walk into the house. The only one who is okay is Josh, and that's because he's away." I wiped the tears from my eyes and tried to see the road. "I've got to get a psychiatric nurse to move in with us, or I have to place him somewhere. I can't do it anymore." I was shaking all over. When we hung up, I realized I was speeding down the turnpike with my emergency brake still on.

Two minutes later, my mom called back. I wiped my tears with my sleeve.

"Beth, you need to talk with Bobbi, who works with me," she said.

"Why?"

"Just talk to her." My mother handed the phone to Bobbi, and she came on the line.

"Beth," said Bobbi, "you have to have him tested for strep."

"He's never had strep," I said.

"You don't know that," said Bobbi.

"Yes I do. I had the records double-checked."

"No," said Bobbi, "you don't know unless you run a blood test. My son suffered like this for ten years before we found out it was all due to strep."

AFTER I HUNG UP with Bobbi, I called my new pediatrician, Dr. Conner Moore. I said it was urgent. He came on the line, and I told him Bobbi's story. He set up a blood test immediately. I collected Sammy from school and drove him directly to the lab. On the way over, I told him Bobbi's story.

Bobbi's son had been diagnosed first with OCD, then with Tourette's. As the years passed, he became more and more violent. He ended up in the juvenile justice system. One day, Bobbi took her daughter to an ear, nose, and throat doctor for a recurrent ear infection. In reviewing the family history, the ENT noted her son's OCD. He mentioned that he had recently been to a medical seminar where one of the panelists had mentioned ongoing research about a possible link between strep and OCD. The ENT did not know much about it, but he wanted to pass the information along. He recommended that Bobbi's son take a blood test for group A strep. It came back positive.

Bobbi's son, like Sammy, had no clinical history of strep—not even a sore throat. Yet his blood test showed that he had strep antibodies raging through his system. According to Bobbi, her son never got better until they started treating him for strep. If strep was the culprit, a blood test was the key.

"Maybe this is it, Sammy; maybe you've got strep. We're going to find out."

I called Chris while I drove. She might have come across this disorder through her work with special needs children.

"Have you heard of this?" I asked. "Mental illness caused by strep."

"No," she said.

I explained what I had learned from Bobbi. "We're on our way to the hospital right now for a blood test," I finished.

"Oh—my—God." She said each word slowly. "Hang on. I'm going online right now to look it up. Yup, here it is. The Web site for the National Institute of Mental Health. I'll read it, keep looking, and send you the links to what I find."

When Sammy and I got to the hospital, we were both excited. He hopped patterns down the hall to the lab and asked a guard to move; she blocked an invisible wall that Sammy needed to scale. The guard would not move, but Sammy shrugged it off and went around her. At the lab, he asked for a moment to compose himself; then he thrust out his arm, took a deep breath, and belted out the song "All Star" from the movie *Shrek*. The lab technician inserted the needle and tapped the vial. It filled with the red liquid from his body that held the answer. I wanted that blood to be drawn from his tiny, dehydrated arm as fast as possible so that we could get the results in a blink.

"When will we know?" I asked the nurse at the desk on our way out.

"Your pediatrician should have the results by eleven tomorrow."

It was a Thursday. Josh was home for his last extended weekend of the school year. I dropped Sammy off with Josh, then drove immediately to my beloved cove. I stood on the edge of the cove, close to the magical place where I had launched my kayak for so many years, and I prayed with all my heart.

I PRAY EVERY DAY. When I wake up in the morning, the first thing I do is thank God for everything good in my life. Even on my worst days with Sammy, I still thanked God for something: food on the table or my friends or the health of my other two sons. There was always something for which I could be grateful. This time was different, though. This time I was asking for something. I asked for the strep test to be positive. Then I had a long talk with God.

I reminded God how I had never prayed for a single material thing, ever, in my entire life. I reminded God how much I had wanted to buy my rental home at the cove but never prayed for it, because I did not think it was right to pray for a possession. I talked about how hard I tried to be a good person and a good mom to my sons. I said I knew I had made a lot of mistakes in life, but still I was always trying. I reminded God how I was helping out by taking good legal care of kids in state custody. I pointed out that I had not whined or complained to God when things had gone poorly for me. I reminded God that I had picked myself up from the depths of depression over my failed marriage and started a new life for my kids and me; that I had never blamed God for anything that had gone wrong, and that all along—no matter how tough things were—I had always believed God was there for me. I repeated all the things that I was grateful for. I thanked God for all the gifts I had been given, for my sons, and for my life in Maine. I said that if God never answered any other prayer of mine, ever again, in my whole life, that would be okay with me if this one prayer of mine could please be answered: that Sammy have strep.

I stood by the water's edge and gazed at the tide and the island. I believed that God heard me and that my prayer would be answered. I believed that with all my heart and soul.

Then I made a promise—not a bargain but a promise. "I promise you," I said out loud, to make sure God heard me, "that if this is what he's got, it will not stop with my son getting better. It will not be that my kid gets better and life goes on. I promise; it will not stop here." I was not sure what I meant when I made that promise. I just knew that I would keep it.

THE NEXT MORNING was a sparkling day in May. I was due at Colony Beach at 11:00 to help with a field trip for James's third-grade class. I was running my typical few minutes late. At 11:02, I called the pediatrician's office en route.

"The doctor's not in," said the nurse. "He's off today, and he's the one who has to give you the results."

I pulled to the side of the road and stopped, less than half a mile from Bradbury's, just past the three-way fork where Wildes District Road splits off from Route 9.

"I've waited too long already," I said. "It's been a year of this, and I need to know the results. Call him at home, do whatever you need to do, but I need those results right now." I choked back tears.

"Hold on," she said.

Please God ran through my head hundreds of times while I waited; then she was back on the line.

"It's four hundred," she said with what sounded like shock in her voice.

"What's that mean?"

"It means he's positive for strep," she answered.

It's hard to believe that there were any more tears inside me, but they gushed out like a waterfall, landing in my lap. Great sobs racked my body and completely took over. My shoulders shook. I lost the ability to speak. All I could think was that God had answered my prayer, that my son was going to be well, and that I now had everything that I could ever want in my life.

"Beth, are you all right? Are you all right?" I heard the nurse's voice asking from what seemed like a faraway place.

"Thank you, God. Thank you, God" was all I managed to say at first. After a while, my brain kicked in and my voice pushed out: "What do we do now?"

"I don't know," I heard her say. "I'm going to call Dr. Moore at home and find out. Will you call me back later?"

"Okay," I managed to squeak out through the sobs. I collected myself as best I could, sucked in a few lungfuls of deep breaths, turned the van around, and headed for home. I tried to let the magnitude of the news sink into my brain.

When I burst through the front door, Josh and Sammy were both in the downstairs den. Josh was on the couch watching television; Sammy was off to the side doing what looked like a tae kwon do move.

"You've got strep!" I cried out to Sammy.

"I've got strep?" He stopped moving and stood perfectly still.

"Yes, baby, you've got strep!" I cried out again. I watched the wheels turn in his head as the information clicked and a grin spread over his face.

"I've got strep!" he repeated with glee.

"Are you serious?" Josh bolted off the couch. His dark eyes were disbelieving.

"He's got it!" I shouted.

"You mean I'm going to get better?" Sammy grinned from ear to ear.

"Yes!" I shouted, not thinking for a minute that recovery was anything but certain. I wanted to pick Sammy up and toss him in the air the way I did when he was little. Instead, I grabbed Josh and hugged him like there was no tomorrow.

Suddenly, I remembered the field trip. "I've got to tell James!" I rushed out to my van and headed to the beach.

COLONY BEACH FRAMES a small, horseshoe-shaped pocket of ocean where the Kennebunk River empties into the Atlantic. When I pulled up and parked, teachers, students, and parents were strung out along the edge of the surf. They were diligently searching for things washed up by the sea. I knew almost everyone there. I was sniffling when I got out of my van and crossed the beach to join them. My feet stepped along, one in front of the other, but I floated somewhere above them. I saw Marty first.

"He's got strep, Marty." I started crying again and hugged her.

Chris, helping at the beach that day, saw us and came over quickly. I reached my hand out to her while I hung on to Marty.

"It's strep, Chris. He's got strep." I watched as the news worked its way through her brain.

"He's going to get better?" she asked, her eyes bulging.

I nodded yes and pulled her into a three-way hug.

Word spread across that beach the way fires whip through the Malibu canyons. Within minutes, I was surrounded by a mob of teachers and moms. Arms reached out and hugged me from every direction. Everywhere I looked, I saw faces full of happy tears.

"He's going to get better. He's finally going to get better!" I sobbed. It was all I could do to remain standing. Judy Hoff, who had taught Josh in grade school, held me up.

"Where's James?" I finally managed to ask.

Marty pointed off toward the end of the beach. I broke away from the crowd and started toward him, calling his name as I went. James charged over to me. I bent down in front of that beautiful face of his, with the golden curls and sea-green eyes. I held his two cheeks gently in my hands.

"Why are you crying?" James asked.

"Tears of joy, sweetie," I said. "Sammy's got strep."

"He's got it! He's got it!" He stepped back and jumped for the sky. "This is the best day of my life! Yaaaa-hooooooooooooo!" he yelled as he took off down the beach at a run, after his friends. He leapt and punched the air with his fist, shouting as he ran. "Yaaaa-hooooo! Yaaaa-hooooo! I don't have to deal with it aneeeeeeeemoooooooore!"

James's friends ran up and surrounded him the same way the moms and teachers had embraced me. I saw them listen for a minute; then they all started whooping and jumping around. I doubted they understood much of what James said, but it wasn't important. Their buddy was unbelievably happy about something, so they were, too. The sun was shining, they were at the beach on a school day, and summer was right around the corner. What could be better when you're eight?

It was good that we basked in that wonderful day of hope and joy and friendship, because the summer did not turn out as we expected.

9

PANDAS

M emorial Day weekend marks the start of summer in
Kennebunkport, as in many towns across the States.
The lawns are mowed. The flowers bloom. The heat is off, and
the windows are open. The shops are full, and the roads are
jammed. There are waiting lists at all the restaurants. Motor-
boats go back in the water. Motorcycles are back on the roads.
Bicyclists meet for early morning rides. Children and parents
flock to Mother's Beach.

The Memorial Day parade strides through Kennebunkport
rain or shine. Fire trucks and Boy Scouts join the bands. Veter-
ans and war nurses wave from convertibles. Bagpipers march
in kilts. The high school band is regal in blue and white. The
band instructor sets the pace, his youngest daughter in tow.
The middle and grade school bands follow, all dressed in black
and white.

I feel proud when James marches past playing his clarinet

next to Marty's daughter Helen. They have been friends since nursery school.

The parade stops for a memorial service on the bridge that crosses the Kennebunk River. The local minister offers a tender prayer. A wreath is dropped gently into the water in memory of those who have died. The crowd is quiet and sad. The parade then returns to Dock Square for a moment of silence and for speeches in front of the monument dedicated "To Our Soldiers and Sailors," erected in 1909. The square overflows with locals and tourists, who press up against the restaurants and shops that line the square. Parents hand water bottles to the students in the bands. If the first President Bush is in town, he gives the opening remarks.

I met him in Colonial Pharmacy one day, a few years before Sammy got sick. The president was talking with the pharmacist about hip surgery. When they hit a lull, I introduced myself.

"You're a very polite boater," I said as I shook his hand.

"Really?" His eyes lit up, his eyebrows lifting.

"Yes. I was kayaking toward the cross-creek one day, and you slowed down when you saw me. Lots of people in bigger boats like yours speed up and cut me off. Not you, though; it was very polite."

"That's good to hear," replied the president with a smile. "I worry about that, always want to be careful."

"Well, you are, so thank you."

On my way out, the Secret Service guy smiled and talked into his wrist. They are always very handsome.

I told Tracy the story while we were kayaking the next day. Somewhat stunned, Tracy said, in her British clip, "You went right up and spoke to a president of the United States—just like that?"

"A good boater likes to be appreciated," I explained.

NEITHER MY PEDIATRICIAN nor I could find any literature directing us on how to proceed. I found a limited number of studies from the National Institute of Mental Health that talked about penicillin, strep, and OCD. The research was less than five years old and concentrated on very young children. Some of it discussed blood procedures that might dilute or eliminate the antibodies. My pediatrician found articles about strep and the fact that it did not develop a resistance to penicillin, which sounded good. Neither of us could turn up a single case study that described how to treat a patient like Sammy.

What we did know was that he had PANDAS, which stands for Pediatric Autoimmune Neuropsychiatric Disorders Associated with Streptococcal Infections. The theory of PANDAS is simple: strep antibodies attack the basal ganglia, which is the area of the brain that controls behavior. In a nutshell, Sammy's brain was under assault.

I called Dr. Drill with the results of the blood test.

"He's got something called PANDAS," I reported. "Do you know about it?"

"I think I read something about that, but I'm not familiar with it," said Dr. Drill.

Dr. Moore decided to start Sammy on 1,500 milligrams of penicillin. He'd take 500 milligrams three times a day while we continued to research. Sammy's daily dose was a whopper. A typical adult dose for strep throat would be 500 milligrams a day, but Dr. Moore felt that the severity of Sammy's illness warranted the larger dose.

Then we did something at which Sammy and I had become experts: we waited to see if the medicine worked.

The day before Josh headed back to school, I rented *Lorenzo's Oil,* a movie about parents who discovered how to treat their son's rare disease. He and I watched it together, after Sammy was asleep, and searched for clues. We could not detect any medical similarities, but the movie's theme boosted our hopes.

Chris offered to help me do research. Late at night, long after our boys were sleeping, we e-mailed articles to each other. We would eventually know as much about PANDAS as perhaps anyone else in the country except, maybe, the researchers at the NIMH. Our lack of medical degrees was a good part of the reason why neither of us felt constrained. We were not bound by traditional medical theories or reasoning. We had everything to gain and nothing to lose. We went for it.

When we started, there were only three things I knew for sure. First, that an antibiotic is useless against a virus. Second, that strep is a bacteria. Third, that I had better understand a heck of a lot more if I wanted my son to get better.

So we dug in.

Years earlier, at Disney World, I had watched and understood a movie about infections. Elisabeth Shue, in a white jumpsuit, starred as an antibody that raced through the bloodstream chasing bacteria. (This was before she was nominated for an Academy Award.) When she found them, she torpedoed them.

The problem is that not all antibodies are as strong as Elisa-

beth Shue. Some bacteria, like strep, are so potent that the antibodies need the help of an antibiotic, like penicillin. Strep
causes quite a few dangerous infections, not just strep throat.

There are two tests to identify strep infections: a throat culture and a blood test. A throat culture will come back positive
or negative. Particularly with children, though, it is possible to
get a false negative. A blood test for strep is more accurate.
Like a blood test for hepatitis, it comes back positive if the patient has ever been infected. A positive blood test also comes
back with a number called the strep titer. The titer tells you
the level of antibodies in the bloodstream; when the titer is
high, it signals a recent infection.

Each patient is different, but when I am in good health, my
blood tests positive for strep with a titer of 100. This is because
I have had a couple of cases of strep throat over the years that
were fully treated, including one on the day when Sammy was
born.

Sammy's blood test had come back positive for strep. This
meant he'd had a strep infection at some point during his life,
even though we never knew it. In medical parlance, Sammy
was "positive for strep with no clinical history." Even more
significant, at 400, his strep titer was elevated.

Within days after Sammy started the penicillin, Chris and
I had located hundreds of articles online. They were highly
technical and hard to understand. I am the type of person
whose eyes glaze over when I read medical information, so for
help deciphering what Chris and I dug up, I turned to my
friend Jim.

Jim lives in Vermont now, but we'd met in California before either of us had children. He grew up in New Jersey and

looks a bit like Ben Stiller. He started his career as a Hollywood writer and director at about the same time I started as a lawyer. We became quick friends after being introduced by family members in Los Angeles.

"I love writing and directing true stories best," he'd said one day. We were getting ready to play tennis on a sunny court cooled by breezes that drifted in from the Pacific.

"How come?" I asked, bouncing a ball on the head of my racket.

"Because they're full of stuff so incredible one would never think to make them up."

Little did I know then how true that would be for me. I reached out to Jim now, not because I thought I had a good story, but because he had been a veterinarian before he became a director. I hoped he could help me with the science.

"Can you explain this to me in plain English?" I asked him in an e-mail, summarizing what was going on as best I could.

He said to think of it as fighting a war.

Infections are enemy bacteria that invade the body. The cell walls of these bacteria are lined with enemy proteins (called antigens). When enemy proteins are detected, the body's immune system sends out billions of antibodies. They are the body's troops. They fight infections by recognizing the enemy proteins and then attacking those cells. Usually it goes smoothly, but sometimes the troops make a mistake. They misidentify a protein and torpedo the wrong cells, causing injuries as if by "friendly fire."

Strep antibodies can be particularly vicious. When they misidentify a protein and attack healthy cells, they can cause permanent liver damage, rheumatoid arthritis, rheumatic fever, scarlet fever, and an involuntary movement disorder called Sydenham's chorea that used to be known as Saint Vitus' dance. In rheumatic fever, strep antibodies go after the heart. In Sammy's case, strep antibodies were mistakenly attacking his brain.

As Chris and I continued to plow our way through the Internet, it became apparent that Dr. Sue Swedo at the National Institute of Mental Health was the leading PANDAS researcher in the country. Dr. Swedo and her team developed the PANDAS theory the same way all brilliant people break through barriers: they made new, creative connections.

They noted the similarities in the behaviors and movements of patients with OCD and patients with Sydenham's chorea. Sydenham's chorea occurs in association with rheumatic fever. Because strep causes rheumatic fever, Dr. Swedo and her team wondered if strep also might be at the root of OCD. They began running studies on children with recurrent strep infections who also suffered from OCD.

Sammy had been on penicillin for about three days when I found Dr. Swedo's e-mail address at the bottom of an article. I wrote her and asked for the protocol for treating a child like Sammy. She e-mailed me back the same day. She was kind, but directed me to studies that suggested that while immediate intervention with penicillin might have helped, the effectiveness waned once the child had exhibited symptoms for more than a few days.

"A few days?" I groaned.

Sammy had been sick for almost a year.

So back to the research we went. But despite all our efforts, we could not find a single study discussing a patient like

Sammy: a child who had no clinical history of strep. I also found it confusing that children were not routinely given strep blood tests the moment they exhibited OCD behaviors. Well-respected doctors at the NIMH had theorized the link; isn't this exactly why taxpayers fund such institutions, to develop cutting-edge medical advice? Could there possibly be a downside to running a blood test?

DR. MOORE'S NURSE called me shortly after I heard back from Dr. Swedo.

"Any improvement?"

"I think there might be, but I'm afraid that the minute I say yes, it will be over."

"What do you notice?" she asked.

"His color is better, he's standing a little straighter, and he seems less stiff when he moves. It's just less trouble for him to get around. Best of all, he hasn't had a crisis for three days."

The absence of crises felt like a vacation. A crisis started out as a low wail that gradually built to a howl, then went to a scream. One crisis-free day was a blessing; three in a row was a miracle.

By the fifth day of penicillin treatment, Sammy had stopped hopping, stopped holding his breath, was no longer murmuring repetitive phrases, and there still had not been a crisis. It felt safe enough for me to take a bike ride. I zipped down to the pier, took a quick look at the lighthouse, then turned around and biked the three miles home. I pedaled into the driveway and nearly fell over. Sammy was outside, sitting on the swing set.

"Mom," he said, smiling, "I'm a boy full of hope."

On the eighth day, I slept late. I woke up when my boys' voices drifted into my room. I groggily lifted my head from the pillow, puzzled over what was bothering me. Then I sat upright and listened intently. "Oh my goodness!" I exclaimed out loud. I could not believe my ears. Sammy's speech pattern had reverted back to the way it used to be. The verbal tics were gone. He *was* getting better!

On the tenth day, Sammy sat on a couch he'd been unwilling to use for almost a year. Then he stood up straight and announced, "I'm going to take a shower." When he finished showering, I heard the hum of his electric toothbrush. I had been cautious about sharing the news of Sammy's possible recovery lest he take a turn for the worst. Now I was excited. I wanted everyone to know! I wanted to stand on the roof and shout at the top of my lungs, "SAMMY'S GETTING BETTER!"

I e-mailed Jim an update: "He's so much better you wouldn't believe it!"

"How much better is he?" he sent back.

"I'd say fifty percent," I typed.

"FIFTY percent?" came across my screen.

"Yes!" I pressed Send.

A moment later, the phone rang. It was Jim.

"You need to call the *New York Times*," he said.

I was never shy about picking up the phone and I remembered my promise to God, so I made two calls that morning: one to the *New York Times* and one to the *Boston Globe*. The *New York Times* reporter called back and left a message about being empathetic but saying that the *Times* was not a social service agency. The *Boston Globe* called back and reached me.

I spoke with Scott Allen, the *Globe*'s assistant editor of the health and science desk, and told him the story.

"I'm forever amazed at the complete lack of coordination between the physical health and the mental health providers," Allen said. Then he asked, "So who do you want to sue?"

"No one."

"You're a lawyer and you don't want to sue anyone?"

"Nope," I said. "I just want to get the story out."

"I'll have a reporter there next week," he told me. "Her name is Carey Goldberg."

After eighteen days on the penicillin, Sammy went back to school. He walked down the hall like every other kid, one foot in front of the other. He did not hunch, hop, or duck. He did not cling to the walls. Teachers, eyes wide with wonder, stopped in the hall and watched him pass. I took some more bike rides and thought about kayaking.

One of my friends e-mailed me: "I just called your house, and Sammy answered. I have to say that he sounded like the old Sammy. He even bantered a bit."

On Day 28, Carey Goldberg came and did the interview. Sammy was excited, expressive, and happy to share his story.

On Day 29, something was different, and it was not good. There was a slight stiffness to Sammy's body movements that I had not seen for weeks. I was determined not to overreact. A day later, when the *Globe* photographer came to take pictures, Sammy was sharp and irritable. We talked to the photographer about different places to take the shot, but we could not find a place that he thought would be comfortable. Finally, we settled on a soft green chair in the television room upstairs. It had been one of his favorite places to sit before he got sick.

"Do you want to put on some lipstick?" the photographer asked me.

"Oh!" I said and hurried upstairs. It had been a long time since I'd thought about makeup. When I came back downstairs with painted lips, she was trying to get Sammy to sit in the chair. Instead of bending at the waist, he threw himself at it like a plank. It was the way he used to throw himself at his middle school locker. My heart sank, but I thought, *Maybe it's just a little dip. Maybe he'll be okay tomorrow. Maybe it's because the* Globe *is here. He's tense, anxious about being in the paper.*

The article ran on the front page of the *Boston Globe* a week and a half later. Within days, the *Globe* reporter was forwarding me hundreds of e-mails from parents all over the country whose children had OCD. Their stories came across my screen for weeks. All were grateful. Some, like me, had accidentally discovered the strep connection. Many were fighting battles with nonbelieving doctors and asked for my opinion on what to do.

"Fire them," I typed back, making a mental note to mail a copy of the article to Dr. Drill. I had not heard from him since the day I'd asked him about PANDAS—not even a quick call to ask about Sammy's progress. I was far too busy to bother calling him. I had no time for doctors who had no time for us.

Other parents e mailed me about their struggles with school systems that thought they were grasping at straws. Some had never heard of anything remotely like a strep connection and were now demanding blood tests. A few reported success from antibiotics. Others wrote about success that came only from blood procedures. One procedure, plasmapheresis, cleansed the blood of strep antibodies. Another, involving a type of immunoglobulin, diluted the antibodies by introducing a pooled blood product. The parents' response was overwhelming.

I shared all of these stories with Sammy. I told him how much he had helped so many other children. I told him how brave and kind he was to share his story.

With my heart in my throat, I told him this first as I watched him walk around awkwardly outside, then while he sat stiffly on a swing. A day later, I watched as he rubbed his feet back and forth on the carpet and—finally—as he lay down on his couch.

I watched . . . and what I saw was that the penicillin had stopped working.

10

Gone Again

Early summer swirled around us. Dock Square, in the center of Kennebunkport, was full of happy tourists. Shops and restaurants overflowed. Bradbury's was packed. Colonial Pharmacy sold sunscreen to tourists. The summer charm of Kennebunkport—the excited tourists, the happy families—was all around us, but it was separate and apart from our existence. We were an island. I visited the pharmacy almost daily for new medicine, and the clogged streets meant more time when I could not be with my son. When I was not driving or caring for Sammy, I was in front of my computer, researching by sunlight and starlight.

He was gone again. I had to get him back.

DURING THE FIRST few days of the decline, when it was apparent that things were going drastically wrong, Sammy forced himself to go to his beloved rocket camp. He raised himself from his couch and dragged himself to the van, with the same sheer force of will that propelled him to math meets.

I drove a double shift. Josh, home for the summer, worked at the camp as a counselor. He and James took the camp bus to Portland. I'd drop them off for the bus, then come home and wake Sammy to drive him to Portland. Each day, it took longer for Sammy to complete his rituals and get into the van. After a few partial days of camp, he collapsed, and his world shrank back to his couch. He was as sick as he had ever been. The Tourette's symptoms had all come back: the tics, the twitches, and the endless throat noises. The compulsions were relentless. The invisible walls cropped up everywhere. The tissues he used to protect his hands when he held an object were strewn about the couch. The floor was scattered with crumbs from the Ritz crackers he crushed into the size and shape of tennis balls. His voice was barely audible when it came through on the walkie-talkie.

This time, though, I knew what I was dealing with, and I was not about to lose my child again. The pediatrician ordered another blood test. Sammy's strep titer was 800.

"Why on earth would it go up?" I e-mailed Jim.

"Shouldn't," he wrote back. "They should go down after the penicillin knocks out the bacteria, and then they should stay down. Maybe it's an infection somewhere in the body that the antibiotics are suppressing but not totally killing off?"

I went back on the Internet. PubMed reported research that showed amoxicillin had a better success rate with strep than penicillin. I faxed my pediatrician the research. He called in a prescription for amoxicillin.

I made a trip to Colonial Pharmacy. Sammy continued his nosedive.

I reached the head of pediatric infectious diseases at a major university in Boston. He doubted that Sammy was still infected with strep and said that strep had no relationship to OCD, but he was willing to work with my pediatrician and treat Sammy as a strep carrier just in case. We began a course of amoxicillin combined with rifampin. There were so many pills, nine pills a day. I was exhausted and had trouble keeping the medication schedule straight. Everything I read emphasized the need for strict compliance. If the label said, "Three times a day," that meant every eight hours would give maximum results. "Two times a day" meant every twelve hours. To keep it straight, I taped a chart to the refrigerator and recorded what pills I gave him and when.

I virtually stopped sleeping. I was on duty around the clock, either giving out pills, researching online, or listening to him pound, jump, and jerk his way around the bottom floor. It took him two hours to get in and out of the bathroom, and that was the only time he left the couch. He had no sleep pattern and was often up until two in the morning. He lay under the couch cushions day and night.

When he did sleep, I often had to wake him up from a dead slumber and give him the pills. His little fingers reached out from under the cushions—like pincers—to take the small pink pottery bowl that held the pills. He had made the bowl for me at camp the year before. There were only two things he would touch without a tissue. One was that bowl. The other was his water glass. He made several stabs in my direction until his fingers successfully latched onto the base of the bowl. Then he chugged the pills like a shot of bourbon, being careful not to let his lips touch the rim. After that, he took one sip from the water glass and handed it back to me.

He got worse. He stopped eating. He balked at taking his meds.

During the daytime, I ministered to Sammy and tried to pay some attention to Josh and James. Late at night and into the wee hours of the morning, I scoured the research I had collected and reread the e-mails I had received from other parents. I tried to find connections. The common theme I detected was that escalating behaviors coincided with an elevated strep titer, independent of any evidence of an active infection. In fact, many of the parents reported that their children had been physically healthy and routinely tested negative on throat cultures, yet blood tests clearly indicated they had been afflicted with strep at some point in the recent past. These children, like mine, had asymptomatic strep. Others routinely had strep throat and often did well on penicillin, but after they stopped the medication, the OCD returned within days.

Based on the e-mails, the research, and what I observed in Sammy, my theory was that his behaviors were worse because of the antibodies. His titer was up; this meant there were more antibodies cross-reacting with cells in his basal ganglia. The literature about OCD referred to a "classic waxing and waning of symptoms." Couldn't the fluctuating antibodies cause the waxing and waning? I faxed this question to a couple of neurologists in Boston but did not get much of a response.

I called the NIMH on a regular basis to get more information and to fill the researchers there in on my latest theories.

They remained polite, but I could tell they were growing weary of me. I did not care. I established that all their studies focused only on penicillin, that there was no research on asymptomatic strep, that blood procedures had been proven to work on young children, and that they had received other reports of children who did well on penicillin for a short time, decompensated, then rallied with a change in medication.

I researched blood procedures. There were two possibilities. We could either remove the antibodies from his blood with plasmapheresis or dilute them with an immunoglobulin. Plasmapheresis is similar to dialysis, and I could not find a hospital anywhere in the country that would do plasmapheresis for a PANDAS patient. An immunoglobulin procedure, or "IV Ig," introduces the pooled blood product of many donors into the bloodstream. For an IV Ig, I needed a pediatric neurologist.

From the parents' e-mails, I located the names of two pediatric neurologists in Boston who were open to the theory of PANDAS and IV Ig for treatment. Their assistants told me, one rudely, that they were booking six months out. I went back online, found the doctors' e-mail addresses, and contacted them directly. I used the *Globe* article to get their attention. One was no longer doing the procedure. The second, who was extremely kind despite his rude assistant, set up an appointment for Sammy for the following week.

I forged forward on the promise to God. I e-mailed Peter Walsh, then the director of the Department of Health and Human Services for the State of Maine. I told him my story. I begged him to have the state issue an advisory to physicians to run strep tests on children presenting with rapid-onset OCD.

One of his key people responded by e-mail: "Could you please clarify something for me. Are you saying that your son had a strep infection and that it caused his mental illness?"

"Yes," I typed back. "Research links strep not only to OCD, but also to anorexia and hair pulling."

It had been eleven days since Sammy's story had graced the front page of the *Boston Globe*.

I FAXED MY PEDIATRICIAN every day to bring him up to date. In one fax, I told him Sammy had screamed in the bathroom for two hours the night before and finally collapsed on the floor from exhaustion. At the bottom, I scribbled, "I am concerned that my approach is logical and therefore I am not conveying how bad it is here. Someone else would be hysterical."

We decided to try another antibiotic: clindamycin. I went back to Colonial Pharmacy.

The clindamycin proved pointless. Sammy was lost somewhere in the recesses of his brain.

We tried twice but never made it to the neurologist in Boston. The first time, Sammy wanted to get a good night's sleep before the appointment, so he made up his mind to sleep in his bed. He spent five hours trying to get himself upstairs. At one in the morning, he gave up, fell into a chair, and collapsed from exhaustion. I called the neurologist's assistant first thing in the morning. I told her, through my tears, what the night had been like. She was furious that we were not going to make the appointment.

"What else could I do?" I asked.

"Be more prepared," she hissed.

I apologized and set up another appointment.

The second time, Chris came over with her husband, Peter, to carry Sammy to the van. Chris would come to Boston with me. The moment Peter picked Sammy up, he started thrashing.

Peter is over six feet tall, so my waif of a child—kicking, punching, and screaming bloody murder—had no chance. Peter carried him out the front door and did his best to gently place Sammy in the van.

Chris and I jumped into the front seats. Peter slammed the van door. We drove away.

"Take me back now!" Sammy yelled.

When he realized we were not turning around, he lurched forward and tried to grab the steering wheel. Chris blocked him. He tried to head-butt her, then flew backward and started kicking. Chris reached for a leg, and he bit her. She let go, and he punched my arm. He tried to scratch us with his nails.

I pulled to the side of the road and sat, shoulders slumped over the steering wheel. Who was this child in my van—the one who raged for twenty minutes and showed no signs of relenting? Where was my son?

"TAKE ME BACK!" he screamed over and over again, before trying to land another punch.

"What shall we do?" I asked as Chris dodged a head butt.

"Sammy, Sammy," Chris said quietly as she held his arm at the wrist, just below a fist. "Your mom is trying to help you."

"I KNOW SHE IS! YOU THINK I DON'T KNOW THAT!" he screamed back, and he threw a punch with his free arm.

"We can't drive with him like this," I said, blocking the punch.

"Probably isn't safe," she agreed, ducking a slap in her direction.

Neither of us wanted to give up, but I pulled the van back into the driveway.

"NOT THAT WAY!" Sammy screamed hysterically.

I pulled out and backed the van into the driveway. Peter carried Sammy out of the van in reverse: feetfirst, backward through the front door, and placed him on the couch just as he'd been before we started.

I walked outside with Chris and Peter.

"I'll have to get an ambulance and sedate him," I said.

They left. I went upstairs, defeated, and called the neurologist's assistant. I told her what we had been through, sharing every detail of that horrific scene. There was momentary silence on the line; then she said:

"Are you telling me you're not coming?"

"Excuse me?" I was confused.

"I said, 'Are you telling me you're not coming?'" Her tone sounded like she wanted to call me a name at the end of the question.

"I'm telling you we can't get there. I'll have to get an ambulance to bring him."

"Do you have any idea how many patients this doctor has?" she asked, launching into assault mode. "Do you realize we scheduled this specifically for you? He is coming here to meet with you, and now you're calling to tell me you're not coming?"

It felt as if she had spit every word, and I lost it.

"Didn't you hear what I said?" I yelled. "My son cannot walk! We carried him to the car. He kicked us. He bit us. He head-butted us. Do you have any idea what it's like to have a child so sick, so hopeless, and there is absolutely nothing you can do? And you're complaining that we didn't make an appointment! What is WRONG with you?!"

I slammed down the receiver, believing that the assistant would answer to a power greater than myself.

Later that day, when Sammy had gained some semblance of stability and I was tending to him, he said, "The next time you wake me up from a dead sleep in a panic and carry me out to the van, at least use the right door."

It was then I realized that our morning disaster was the first time Sammy had been through the front door in a year.

11

Inside Looking Out

Me

If I thought about it, if I had the time, I would feel sorry for myself.

The tears that I'm crying would be for me, not for him, because my life is so sad—to feel so alone and so pressured, with every minute being scheduled or demanded.

I look in the mirror, and I see a stranger. I look at green eyes that used to sparkle back. All I see is sadness and exhaustion. If I look long enough, they fill with tears, but I don't have time to look. I am in a constant state of motion. I'm dispensing meds, or ordering meds, or trying to remember something about the meds. I'm e-mailing doctors and asking questions. I'm trying hard not to scream at them with the words I type. I call my friends and sob, but not for me. I sob for him: that life could be so unfair, that he could be so brilliant and so trapped.

Then he calls to me and I go to him, and I know that I will lie again and tell him there is hope.

He stands there with his eyes shut and his fists clenched. He is rubbing his feet back and forth on the carpet. He wants something, maybe something to drink or Ritz crackers to crush. Tears are streaming down his cheeks.

I kick myself for taking the time to dry my own tears before running to him. Maybe if I had been here sooner, or had brought the crackers with me, or had woken him earlier, or let him sleep later, or had done a thousand things a different way, then maybe he wouldn't be crying right now. And it's my fault again for buying the house, for moving from the beach, for getting married, for getting divorced, for not feeding him the right kind of food.

There has to be a reason.

He points his face toward me, and he says while he cries, "Mom, I have such a sad life. Don't I have a sad life, Mom?"

I muster all the conviction I can, and I say, "Sammy, we are going to figure this out. We're going to try a new medicine, and you are going to get better. It's going to take us a while more, but we are going to get there. I promise you."

"But, Mom, what if we don't"—he pauses—"get there?"

He says this with tears making tracks on his cheeks. The cheeks I want to take between my hands and smother with kisses filled with love. The kisses that will push away the hurt. The cheeks I cannot touch, or he will have to do another round of compulsions. The cheeks I love with all my heart, with every inch of me, because they are my darling son's, and it is killing me to see him in such pain.

"Sammy, we will get there. I promise. We will figure this out, and we will get there."

I am standing there saying things to him that I'm not sure I believe. I want to believe what I'm saying, but I just don't know anymore. I have to believe it, though, for him.

I get him whatever he needs. Then I head back upstairs to make more phone calls, and e-mail more doctors, and read more articles. And I stop crying, because there is so much more work I have to do.

As I climb the steps to my office, I thank God for my intelligence, for my computer, for the Internet, for my pediatrician, for my children's schools, for my friends, and for sending us the *Globe* reporter. I remind myself of all the good things in my life.

Josh

I DON'T THINK he's going to get better. Before I thought that he would, but not anymore. And I don't know why he can't stop doing all that stuff he does. It's horrible here. I just want to go back to school.

James

"Who do you think is the unluckier one, me or Sammy?" I asked Mom at the bus stop.

She said, "What do you think?"

I told her it was me. I feel like, "Why did it have to be ME that was the one that ended up with a brother that had an excessive-compulsion disorder?"

Why couldn't—it just seems like—it's a one-in-a-million chance that this would happen—so why did it have to be me? It makes me feel bad. It makes me feel bad for Sammy. It makes me feel unlucky because I am in this position. And also it makes me just feel, like, so sad.

He cries in the bathroom, once a day, for like three hours, every single day. It is LOUD; screaming. I remember when this all first started. I was seven. Sometimes, it would be in the middle of the night and I'd hear some thumping, and I'd go out. I'd see Sammy walking around everywhere with his eyes closed, feeling everything. I didn't really say anything to him. I think I mentioned something to Mom, not sure. It was kind of weird.

I have sessions where I talk to the teachers about it. So all the teachers know everything about it. I told some of my friends a little bit about it. But I don't tell them a lot about it, or anybody else.

I can't have any of my friends over.

Sammy makes this weird throat sound where he goes like, "Ehhhh. Ehhhh." He never goes anywhere. And, um, he never wears any socks with his shoes, so his feet smell really, really bad. And if anybody doesn't wear shoes, he will, like, go crazy and get really mad.

One day me and Mom were going to the movies. Mom was really frantic because Josh was home. And she thought Josh might yell at Sammy to stop, and then he'd have a crisis, and we'd be in the middle of the movie. And we'd be like half an hour away. And she was saying all this stuff. And then she turned the car around and we went back home. Ebert and Roeper said it was a good movie.

At dinner, and at other times, he's like, "Puuuuuutttt, puuuuuuttt." "Puuuuuutttt, puuuuuuttt." "Puuuuuutttt, puuuuuuttt." "Puuuuuutttt, puuuuuuttt." "Puuuuuutttt, puuuuuuttt." "Puuuuuutttt, puuuuuuttt." And he just sits there doing that. And it is very bothering. It is just sooooooooo annoying.

One time I just kinda said, "Mom, can you remember when Sammy wasn't sick?" And she didn't really say anything.

Sometimes I had to be the messenger, very annoying. Because whenever Sammy needed something, if I was downstairs, I'd have to go and tell Mom. It kept happening; very annoying to me. Now we're using my walkie-talkies. It's a good thing I got those for my birthday.

I wish she'd get married again. He could help. While she was doing work, he could take care of Sammy. Or while he was out doing work, she could take care of Sammy. It would help.

I wish she'd get me a dog; then I wouldn't feel so alone.

Sammy

DAY AFTER DAY I lie on this couch, and night after night I seep beneath the cushions for warmth. Many times I wonder if death is an easier choice.

12

Stomach Ulcers

The white frame building that housed my pediatrician's office must have been built in the fifties. The small windows and vinyl furniture spoke of a different time and place. Dwarfed by Southern Maine Medical Center and surrounded by the chain stores that had sprung up along Route 1, the office felt like a haven in a storm.

I was almost at the breaking point. Sammy had experienced that brief glimmer of normalcy, then retreated to the dark hollows of his mind. He had finally lost all hope. With the exception of my pediatrician, all the doctors I'd contacted in the greater New York–Boston area had told me that I was wrong about strep being the cause of my son's disorder. We had tried penicillin, amoxicillin, amoxicillin with rifampin, and clindamycin. He was worse than ever, and I was scared that maybe we had run out of options.

"Don't give up," Dr. Moore said, and then he told me a story about stomach ulcers.

"When I was in medical school, we were cauterizing ulcers, giving all sorts of medication, suggesting diet changes, stress eliminators, what have you. We were even excising parts of stomachs. One doctor said he thought it was bacterial, and that stomach ulcers could be cured with antibiotics. Everyone thought he was wrong. Twenty years later, he won the Nobel Prize in medicine."

"So you're saying if I keep going, we might win the Nobel Prize?" I sniffled and smiled.

"Wouldn't that be something?" he chuckled.

I will never forget that conversation. It put me back up on the horse.

"WHO TREATED YOUR SON?" I was on the phone to Bobbi again. It was July. Six weeks had passed since Bobbi had first told me about PANDAS.

I'll never know for sure why it didn't occur to me to make that call earlier. Maybe I needed the heartbreaking frustration of being within reach of saving my child, of knowing the answer was out there, but hitting a brick wall at every turn. Maybe I needed doctors to tell me that I was wrong when I absolutely knew I was right and for that neurologist's assistant to insult me for failing where there could be no success. Perhaps I needed all of that to happen so that I would know how much strength and courage it takes to keep going in the face of overwhelming odds. If it had happened too easily, I might not have understood the importance of continuing to share our story.

Bobbi gave me the telephone number for Dr. Catherine Nicolaides, a developmental pediatrician in Marlton, New Jersey. When I called her office, it was closed for Fourth of July weekend. I searched the Internet and came up with the mailing address. I copied the article from the *Boston Globe,* wrote a three-page letter outlining Sammy's history, and then Express Mailed the package to her. If she had helped Bobbi's son, perhaps she might be able to give my pediatrician direction in terms of what we should be doing. My letter asked her to consult on Sammy's case.

I sent the same package to the Elmwood Pediatric Group in Rochester, New York. Elmwood had done a lot of the PANDAS research I had reviewed on PubMed, and the practice was mentioned in the *Globe* article. One of the doctors from Elmwood called me within a day.

"Since he's been sick for so long," she said, "we have no idea how to treat him. Our experience is with catching it within a day or two of the onset of symptoms."

"Do you know anyone who would know how to treat him?"

"No. I wish I did, but I don't."

Dr. Nicolaides was on vacation when my package arrived, so it took a few days to reach her. The conversation I had with her when we did connect is forever etched in my mind.

She confirmed that she had treated Bobbi's son.

"I think your son's on the wrong antibiotic," she said next. "In my experience, the children respond to Augmentin."

I zeroed in on the word "children."

"You've treated more than Bobbi's son?" I gulped.

"Oh, yes." She had a pleasant, almost singsong voice.

"How many more children with this have you treated?" I was breathless.

Dr. Nicolaides consulted with her nurse for a moment before she answered; then she said, "Twelve or thirteen."

I could not believe my ears. This doctor had treated more PANDAS patients with antibiotic therapy than any other practitioner in the entire country. She didn't just study them; she *treated* them.

"Did they all get better?" I heard myself ask in a disbelieving voice, almost afraid to hear the answer.

"Oh yes," she said in her soft voice.

I prayed before I asked the next question. "Are you saying my son will get better?"

"Oh . . . he'll get better," she said.

With those four words the earth stopped spinning, gravity took a leave of absence, and time stood still. Great waves of emotion swept over me. I choked back tears.

"It will take a long time," she added, "but he'll get better."

I QUICKLY DISMISSED the idea of a consultation and set up an appointment for two weeks away. We needed time to get him healthy enough to get there. I put together a chart showing Sammy's medication history and faxed it to Dr. Nicolaides. She had agreed to review it and suggest medication changes to our pediatrician, pending our visit to her.

She called me in short order.

"I had no idea he was on Zoloft," she said. "In some children, the SSRIs can make it worse. They can increase the behaviors."

This was exactly what I had asked Dr. Drill two months

earlier at Sammy's request. Dr. Nicolaides wanted Sammy to stop taking Zoloft. She also wanted him to start taking 500 milligrams of Augmentin twice a day.

Weaning Sammy off the Zoloft was a double-edged sword. Usually, it's done slowly over a period of weeks or months. Otherwise, the body can go haywire, like with a heroin addict going cold turkey. In Sammy's case, his behaviors were so extreme—and his situation so desperate—that we accelerated the weaning process to as fast as seemed safe. Within a week, he was off the Zoloft. Dr. Nicolaides, working with Dr. Moore, prescribed Gabitril, a mood stablizer.

By then it was too painful for Sammy to wear clothing. He lay on the floor of the den, under a sheet, emaciated. Scattered about him were the hundreds of tissues he used whenever he wanted to touch something. His internal clock was completely off. Mine was, too. Day and night were distinguished only by whether the sun was up.

At two o'clock one morning, I waited helplessly in the den, listening as he pounded, banged, and howled behind the bathroom door. Three hours later, dripping with sweat, he got himself out of the bathroom and over to the couch.

"Can I get you anything?" I asked, my heart torn to pieces.

"No. I just want to gloat over the enormous victory of getting out of the bathroom."

THE CHILDREN'S PATERNAL GRANDMOTHER visited. I had told her what was going on, but seeing it was another matter. She was horrified and took me aside.

"Beth, I want to help. How about if I pay for your health insurance?" she asked.

"That would be wonderful," I said gratefully.

"Have the bills sent directly to me," she said, nodding gravely.

AS BADLY AS Sammy needed me, there were times when it was unbearable for me to spend another minute with him. If he didn't seem close to crisis, if the tide was right and Josh was home to keep an eye, I'd call my co-adventuress in kayaking.

"Jill, can you meet for a quick kayak?" I'd ask, giving her ten minutes' notice.

If she could, I'd rush to meet her.

Jill lives at the top of the road where we had rented our house by the cove. Easily six inches taller than I am, she is the most athletic of my friends. She bought a kayak shortly after I introduced her to the sport. Jill always has a lot going on with her family, her spinning classes, her book club, the college courses she sometimes takes for fun, and her work at Tom's of Maine. But with a few minutes' notice, if she had the time, I could depend on Jill to go kayaking with me. She is a stronger skier and a faster cyclist, but at kayaking I've always led the way.

In years past, we'd paddled out to the ocean where the swells were so big that, if we were in the dip, we'd sometimes lose sight of the coastline. We'd paddled to a nearby island to visit the seals. We'd spotted rainbows that dipped into the sea after a quick summer shower.

"Some people spend the whole year waiting for their one week in Maine. We get to be here all the time!" Jill said as we paddled lazily one summer afternoon.

We'd just ridden the tide into Cape Porpoise Harbor, and the water was thick with feeder fish. They'd leapt from the sea and onto our boats to escape the snapping jaws of the stripers. As we used our paddles to push them out of our boats, we giggled so hard that we cried.

This year, the tears were different. I told her how sad it was at home. I cried for Sammy—that he'd been so brilliant, that he'd been misdiagnosed so long ago, and that it seemed hopeless. Sometimes Jill cried, too. When I ran out of tears, we paddled back, and I hurried home to be with him again.

MY FIRST CONCERN ABOUT going to New Jersey was how to get Sammy into the van. I could not risk another disaster, as when we had tried to get him to the neurologist in Boston. I inquired about a sedative, but Dr. Nicolaides said it would do her absolutely no good to see him sedated. He would have to walk himself to the van and cooperate on the ride. In order for that to happen, I needed help from Josh and James.

The three of us stood on the upstairs porch so that Sammy would not be able to hear us talk.

"If he knows the point of the trip is to see a doctor," I began, "he might not be willing to go, so we have to pretend we're going on a vacation." I spoke softly, just in case a window might be open. "I know the last thing you want to do is take a long car trip, but we all have to go. Especially Josh—if he thinks Josh is staying home, he'll balk."

Josh nodded solemnly in agreement.

"Will we stay at a hotel?" James asked, eyes wide with excitement.

I nodded yes.

"With a pool?" He could barely contain himself.

I nodded yes.

"And a Jacuzzi?" He jumped with enthusiasm.

"If I can find one."

"WE'RE TAKING A VACATION!" I announced later that day, bursting into the den.

Sammy was on the couch, under the cushions. Josh and James were watching television.

Josh looked up. "That's great, Mom," he exclaimed on cue.

"It will do us good to get away," I added cheerily.

James jumped up and shouted, "Where are we going?"

"New Jersey. I found a great hotel there, with a swimming pool and a Jacuzzi."

James hopped up and down in circles. "Yippeeee!"

"And while we're there," I added casually, "we'll stop by and see a doctor who might be able to help Sammy."

Sammy stared at me silently from under his cushions.

A COUPLE OF DAYS before we left, I faxed Dr. Nicolaides that it had been five consecutive days since Sammy had a crisis. On the day I sent that fax, Sammy had been on the Augmentin for ten days and the Gabitril for seven. This was his longest crisis-free period since his brief rally when Dr. Moore had first prescribed penicillin. Dr. Nicolaides wanted to update the blood work before we left. It had been a month since the test that showed the strep titer had climbed to 800. She wanted a complete workup in case we needed to be concerned about anything else. In addition to the strep titer, the prescription for the blood work included lots of other tests: glucose, liver profile, ceruloplasmin, thyroxine, anti-DNase B, EBV panel, lead, CRP, CBC with diff, mononucleosis, and Lyme disease.

The blood work required a trip to the hospital. The van was parked on the side lawn, just steps from the house.

"Sammy, we have to go to the hospital. There's no other way to do this," I said.

"I know, Mom," he answered from the couch. "I'm trying to move. I'm going to. I just need more time."

Three hours later, I said I would call an ambulance. When I picked up the telephone, he was out the door and in the van in one rapid motion.

At the hospital, I offered him a wheelchair to get to the lab, but he wanted to walk the long hall that took us there. When they called his name and he dragged himself into the chair, I sighed with relief, but the worst was yet to come. Sammy's arms were so withered from lack of food and drink that two lab technicians could not find a vein. He bravely tried to sing "All Star," as he had for previous tests. But after lots of random prods and false starts, he was sobbing, and I took charge.

"No more!" I boomed. "I want the best lab tech you have. No one touches him until then."

His pained eyes were full of apologies. "I'm causing so much trouble," he cried.

"No, you're not, baby, I'm just so sorry you have to go through this." I cried, too. It was unbearable. "I love you so much, sweetheart. I'd do it for you if I could."

Finally, a pediatric blood technician came to help. She took one look, explained that he was dehydrated, and had him start drinking water. Two hours later, she suctioned the blood from his veins to fill the vials. He sobbed and screamed. I watched and cried and bit my lip. Then, thank God, it was over.

During those weeks while we waited for him to get well enough to travel, I faxed Dr. Nicolaides with behavioral updates, especially when there were glimmers of hope. The verbal tics and lip smacking were gone. He answered the telephone twice. He tried for two hours to get himself off the couch for a trip to the beach, but finally gave up. Even though he was no longer bathing, he tried—unsuccessfully—to brush his teeth. One day, he played a board game with his brothers. These were milestones.

I woke repeatedly during the night to track his sleep pattern. Once he fell asleep, which happened between three and four-thirty in the morning, he slept for ten to fourteen hours. He insisted on taking the Gabitril at exactly eleven every night. I wondered if it might be keeping him up, and I wanted to switch it.

"Sammy, I'm having you take the Gabitril at four P.M. today."

He looked at me with utter shock. "But, Mom, I need at least a day's notice to make a change like that."

The most important thing was that he was eating and drinking again. I happily served spaghetti and meatballs at three in the morning. He was proud when he showed me that he had finished a full twenty-ounce bottle of water. My heart warmed when he curled up on his couch, with a full stomach, and finally drifted off to sleep.

On the morning of our departure, I parked the van at the side door again. It took him two hours to get from the house into the van, but he made it, and we were off. Josh was in the passenger seat, beside me. James was in the middle. Sammy, immobile, was stretched flat across the bench seat in the back.

THE LONG CAR RIDE from Maine to South Jersey with three kids is always challenging, but this trip gave new meaning to that word. Sammy stayed in the van for the bathroom breaks we made in Massachusetts and New York. We had just crossed into New Jersey when I heard murmuring from the back.

"Did someone say something?"

"It was Sammy. He needs to use the bathroom!" James shouted.

"You don't need to shout, James," I called back tiredly.

"Well, you couldn't hear him!" James shouted again.

"I couldn't hear because he didn't speak up. I can hear you."

There was more murmuring.

"Did he say something else?" I asked.

"He needs to go right away!" James shouted again.

"James, stop shouting!" Josh yelled.

"Josh, don't yell at James." My inner mom let loose.

"I can't hear the music." Josh pointed to his ears.

"Fine, we'll turn the music up." I reached for the radio.

"Then you'll never hear him!" James shouted.

"James, stop it!" yelled Josh.

"Mom, Sammy said to tell you he has to go RIGHT NOW!" James shouted his loudest.

"I'm looking for an exit!" I yelled toward the back.

I zipped off at the next exit and into the potholed parking lot of a run-down, one-story building. Its dilapidated sign announced its name as "The Moonlight." I went in first to make sure the place was okay. It smelled bad and the carpets were torn up, but it looked to me like no one would die there. I got permission to use the bathroom as long as we all bought Cokes.

Back at the van, I said, "It's not the best place, Sammy. It doesn't smell good in there. Should I keep looking?"

"No, it'll be okay. I have to go."

"Does anyone else want to use the bathroom?" I asked.

"I'm not going in that place." Josh turned his nose up.

"Me neither," said James.

Twenty minutes later, Sammy had twisted his way out of the van. Josh and James and I sat there, sucked on our Cokes, and watched. We were not allowed to help. Every time a person entered or exited the Moonlight, Sammy had to start all over again from the beginning. He finally made it into the lobby, where he hopped and swirled around for a while; then he headed back out to the van without ever making it into the bathroom.

"Oh God," Josh and I groaned in unison.

"What happened?" James asked.

I left Josh to answer and met Sammy halfway across the parking lot.

"It smells bad in there," he said.

"I told you it smelled bad."

"Not that bad," he said.

"Look, there's a tree. You could go over there." I pointed to three scrawny bushes on the side of the parking lot in full view of every passing car. One half-dead tree stood lopsided in the middle of the bushes.

"No." He shook his head. "Let's go somewhere else."

"Sammy, I don't know how long that will take. Use the tree."

"Mom, I'll wait."

I knew better than to try to persuade Sammy, so I slid open the van door and waited.

After another twenty or so minutes of various gyrations, he was back in the van. For the next thirty minutes—which felt like two hours—I frantically searched for a better place; I eventually found a McDonald's. Apparently there is an exception that permits reduced compulsions in the event of bathroom emergencies at McDonald's. He made it inside in a heartbeat. Getting out of the bathroom was different; there was no exception. His brothers and I waited it out on the plastic molded seats attached to the generic tables. Josh and James played with their Game Boys. I focused on being grateful for McDonald's.

"Go check on your brother," I periodically instructed Josh while I ate another French fry.

"Still in there," he'd report back.

"How far?"

"About halfway out."

After another hour or so, Sammy was out, in the van, and we were back on the road.

TWELVE OR SO HOURS after leaving Maine—at that point, who's counting?—we pulled up in front of our vacation spot: the Summerfield Suites. Josh and James and I staggered out of the van like zombies. Sammy stayed in it while I went in to see about the room. From the lobby, while I checked us in, I could see that the pool and Jacuzzi looked decent.

"Here you go. Nice second-floor room, views of the pool," the clerk said cheerily as she handed me the key.

"Thank you." I took the key and asked wearily, "Where's the elevator?"

"We don't have one," said the clerk with a smile.

"You don't have an elevator?" I was stunned. It had not occurred to me that hotels without elevators existed in the new millennium. Without an elevator, how would Sammy reach the second floor?

"No elevator," she said politely.

"Can we get a room on the first floor?" I was panicked.

"We're completely booked," the clerk told me, still smiling.

"He'll never make it," said Josh impatiently.

Assuming that positive thinking could only help, I insisted that Josh and I each lug a heavy suitcase up the outside staircase to the room. Josh gets prickly when I persist in doing things like this.

"He's not going to make it, Mom," Josh repeated as I opened the door and shoved a suitcase inside.

Then I stood at the top of the staircase and visualized Sammy struggling to make it upstairs.

"Yup," I sighed deeply and pulled the suitcase back out.

"Told you so," said Josh.

We trudged down the stairs and loaded the suitcases back into the van. I explained to the hotel clerk that we would not be able to stay at the Summerfield Suites, that my son was too ill to climb the stairs to the room, and that we had no choice but to leave. The clerk graciously refunded the room fee in full.

I pulled out my trusty AAA guidebook and searched. My former criteria had been pool and Jacuzzi. Now it was pool, Jacuzzi, and elevator. I made a few calls, realized there were open rooms available everywhere that were accessible by elevator, and we started off again. At the first few hotels, I gamely parked, got out, and walked in to check it out myself. They were all rejects. Either the pool was crummy, the Jacuzzi did not allow kids, or there was simply too much cement. The one that looked good had just booked the last room moments before our arrival. The clerk promised to call if he got a cancellation.

Eventually, we pulled up to the Doubletree Guest Suites in Mount Laurel. Exhausted, I sent Josh and James in to scope it out and report back to headquarters.

"Make sure there's an elevator," I wearily called after them.

They came back with giant smiles.

"They've got elevators, and it's really nice," Josh said happily.

"Kids can use the Jacuzzi!" James nodded excitedly.

I slogged into the lobby and felt relieved when they said they had a room for two nights. I felt even more relieved when I looked over my shoulder and noticed a bar. The clerk handed Josh and James each a thick, warm chocolate chip cookie. She pointed me to the elevator. I took the keys to our second-floor suite at the back of the hotel, and then I went to get Sammy.

Josh piled our bags on a large moving cart while Sammy started his safari from the van to the room. A new, complex movement had popped up just before we'd left home. It was a shuffle, peppered with swirling legs and hopping, all in one motion.

I manned the halls and the elevator, urging the hotel staff and the other guests to leave him alone. Everyone wanted to help this boy who was in such obvious distress, but the slightest offer of help caused him to start the entire process again.

He was in a solid sweat from the extreme physical labor of all the movements.

More than two hours later, Sammy had made it from the van to the hotel room. The route might ordinarily take ten minutes.

Then, in a strange twist, he went immediately into the shower and stayed under the running water for a good half hour. He had me toss him a bathing suit. He put it on, went to the pool with a minimum of compulsions, and threw himself into the water with Josh and James.

Instead of trying to make sense of this, I went to the bar and got a brandy.

13

The Angel Came

I was born in the fifties. I grew up in South Jersey, where there were basically two seasons: green and gray. On summer nights, the humidity hung around and made me stick to my sheets. The winters were cold with no snow.

My mother had wanted to grow up to be a war nurse and save hundreds of soldiers' lives, but her parents would not permit it. She became a teacher instead. My dad, an engineer, sold bottling machinery to beverage companies like Pepsi-Cola and Bacardi. He traveled quite a bit, and he came back from winter business trips to Puerto Rico with suntanned arms from golfing.

I have two distinct memories from when I was little. One is when my dad lifted me onto his shoulders so I could get a better view of a rainbow. I was about five, and I told him that I'd remember it for the rest of my life. He said maybe not, because some things we forget when we grow up. Every day for months,

I reminded myself about that rainbow, until I knew that I would not forget. The other memory is of watching my mother in an emergency room when I was about seven. We had been at the Philadelphia Zoo when my littlest sister fell and cut her head. My grandmother kept us to the side, while my mother argued with the doctors. They wanted to whisk my sister off alone to stitch her up. My mother stood her ground.

"I will not leave my baby," she insisted, head held high, and I knew that was how it would be.

We lived in a development of houses that looked mostly the same. Me, my brother and sisters, and our friends, we ran free all over the neighborhood. We played tag and kickball and capture the flag. I was the oldest of my siblings. I was short and skinny with freckles, and I was bossy. I did not spend a lot of time thinking about being a girl. What mattered most to me was that I ran just as fast as the boys and could play just as well. When we played in teams, I was always a captain. When I was "it," you were probably going to lose.

I liked to watch television. My father nicknamed me Teresa (for T) Veronica (for V), because I spent so much time in front of the TV watching old movies. I liked all the glamorous dancing and singing. I liked *Perry Mason,* too. Because of that show, I decided to become a lawyer. It never occurred to me to be his secretary, Della Street—never even crossed my mind.

I got interested in boys about the same age as everyone else and spent a lot of time concerned about the sweep of my hair. I made all my own skirts because I wanted Villager sets, and they were expensive. I had a wild crush on a boy whose mother told me that I needed to dumb it down. She thought I should pretend I needed help opening my locker. I was never any good at that sort of thing.

At the heart of it, I am a Jersey girl: what you see is what you get.

"HE'S GOT A TREMOR."

Those are the first words Dr. Nicolaides spoke to us in her South Jersey office. She held his file. It had taken her less than two minutes to make that assessment as she looked back and forth from him to the open file. No one else had ever mentioned the word "tremor."

She's the one, I heard from my head and my heart.

I had not met an angel in person before. I had known their presence, but this one was human, with a medical degree and children of her own. She had long, dark, flowing hair and coffee-colored eyes as big as saucers. She wore a dress and high heels. She looked polished. When she walked in, my impression was that she would fit in at a studio meeting. I remembered back to a time when I used to look like that—put together—before Sammy was sick and I was ragged.

Sammy, still in his bathing suit, had finally managed to clamber onto the examination table, where he squirmed, stiff and uncomfortable. His chin was slightly lifted. Through slitted eyes, he watched her suspiciously. His scabbed, frail limbs stuck out like chicken legs. He wore the same filthy, long-sleeved navy polo he had been in for weeks. His hair was tangled and greasy, but he was cleaner than usual due to the shower and pool.

It had taken him over an hour to get from the hotel room

to the van, then another hour to get out of the van and into the doctor's office. I was surprised when we pulled up. I had expected something gleaming and white or imposing and concrete. She was, after all, the foremost PANDAS practitioner in the country. Instead, it was an unassuming, two-story brown wooden office building located in what felt like farmland.

It had been a tough night. I'd lain awake in the bedroom of the suite and listened to Sammy pound, jerk, rub, and jump until three in the morning. When he fell quiet, I shut myself in the bathroom and sobbed. I cried for the son I had lost, for the mothers of sons in Iraq, for the pain of mothers all over the world. My son was asleep on the other side of the bathroom door, yet he was gone.

She's our only hope, I thought silently as I watched her.

"Can you see the tremor," she asked, "in his hand?"

I shook my head no. A tremor is an involuntary muscle movement. Maybe I was just too exhausted, but when I looked at him, all I could see was overwhelming sickness.

"I think he has serotonin syndrome," the angel said next, "from the Zoloft."

She said it might be responsible for a number of his problems, including the tremor. It may have caused too much serotonin to be in his system. According to the research I did later, if it is extreme enough, serotonin syndrome can cause death. Thank goodness we weaned him when we did.

I gave her the historical overview, supplementing the facts I had put in my letter and faxes. I covered the declining year, his consistent brilliance at math meets, his crises, his short recovery, and then the dramatic decline that ended with his valiant but unsuccessful attempt to go to rocket camp.

"Face it, Mom. I'm a failure," Sammy interrupted.

"You're not a failure, Sammy," I corrected. "You're not well, and that's why we're here."

He was not able to tolerate a physical examination. He bristled at even the most gentle, unobtrusive touch. After a couple of careful attempts, mostly gentle taps with a little hammer to test reflexes, the angel realized it was fruitless. She stood back and looked at his emaciated, twitching, scabbed, and bruised body. She said that plasmapheresis, one of the blood procedures I'd researched, would be our absolute last resort, but she wanted me to continue to explore its availability.

"You have to stay nearby for a week," she said. "I need to see him again to assess what to do next." Then she added Zyprexa to the medication mix and floated out of the room.

I made our next appointment with her assistant. Sammy made his way through the maze of obstacles his compulsions required to get out of her office and back to the van.

Sammy was the sickest PANDAS patient Dr. Nicolaides had ever seen.

THE POOL AT THE Doubletree Guest Suites in Mount Laurel is located in the center of a beautiful courtyard with manicured lawns that are framed by the hotel. The first-floor rooms each have a small patio that faces the lawn. From those rooms, the guests can walk directly across the lawn and out to the pool. There are a couple of picnic tables on a large patio at one end of the pool. Since we needed to stay for a week, we needed a first-floor room. I had to be able to pace the lawn, keep an eye on the kids, and make calls about blood procedures while I was out of Sammy's hearing range.

Moving rooms was a two-part process. First I had to arrange for the room; then I had to get Sammy there. Josh waited in the van with Sammy while I went to make the arrangements. James came with me.

"Can I help you?" The clerk stepped to the chest-high counter. She wore a navy blazer and looked at me over the top of her tortoiseshell reading glasses.

"I hope so. We're scheduled to check out tomorrow, but my middle son is sick. The doctor wants us to stay for a week," I explained.

"We can do that," she said, looking at her computer screen.

James, at my side, kept jumping up to try to see the clerk.

"Could we possibly move to a first-floor room facing the courtyard? I need to keep an eye on him in the pool." I pointed to James as the top of his blond head momentarily bounced into view.

"The Jacuzzi, too!" James added at the top of a bounce.

The lovely clerk tapped on her keyboard. "We'll find one for you."

"Do we get another cookie, since it's a new room?" James shouted up mid-bounce.

She leaned over and handed him a few.

I went out to the van and told Sammy about the new room.

"First I have to go back to the old one," he said.

"No, you don't. Josh and I will move everything."

"I have to go there first."

"How come?" I asked foolishly.

He did not answer, and I did not ask again.

I helped Sammy out of the van. James sat in the lobby and ate chocolate chip cookies. I reviewed the "do not move from

this couch, scream 'stranger' if anyone comes near you" protocol. The clerk said she would watch out for him. Sammy started
his tortured way through the halls. Josh and I went to the old
room, repacked the suitcases, loaded up a rolling cart, and
moved everything to the new room. Once we were moved in,
Josh and James went to the pool. I surrendered myself to reading
the volumes of research I'd brought with us and kept a periodic
eye on Sammy as he shuffled, leapt, and jerked his way along the
halls. My California Spanglish saved me with the maids.

"*Mi niño está muy enfermo. No está preocupado. Por favor, no
habla con el.* It'll be okay." My boy is very sick. Don't be concerned. Please, don't talk to him. It'll be okay.

Three or four hours later, Sammy—dripping with sweat
from completing all his compulsions—had been back to the
old room and then arrived at the new one. He collapsed on
the couch and, except for trips to the bathroom, did not leave
it for the next two days.

DURING THE WEEK, I paced the lawn and dialed. Sammy, in
his navy polo and bathing suit, lay on the couch and watched
television. James cycled happily from the room to the pool to
the Jacuzzi. The place was mobbed with families, so there
were endless pool games. Josh, either with his nose buried in a
book or playing with his Game Boy, sat by the pool and
helped me keep track of James. The mall was five minutes
away, so I dropped Josh and James off for daily excursions to
wander the shops or see a movie.

"You have to stay side by side the whole time," I told
them. "Are we clear about that?"

They nodded yes.

"And Josh is in charge; what he says goes—no arguing. Otherwise, this isn't going to work." I looked directly at James, who nodded yes.

I spent a lot of time on the telephone with the NIMH, looking for treatment advice. We did not see eye to eye on Sammy's condition, because he did not fit three of its five diagnostic criteria for PANDAS. The NIMH wanted onset at an earlier age, episodic (not constant) behaviors, and a positive throat culture for strep.

"How could we have a positive throat culture if we never knew he had strep?" I asked the nice researcher. "My son is asymptomatic. Maybe the criteria are wrong?"

When I felt them grow weary of me, I called my former brother-in-law, a doctor. Divorce had not stopped my children's paternal family from being supportive. He agreed to call the NIMH. He did not necessarily support my PANDAS theory, but he was willing to do whatever he could to help. He got the staff talking to me again.

What I came to understand is that diagnostic criteria are established in the context of research studies. Research studies are approved because the criteria and goals are specific. Sammy did not fit the criteria for the research studies; but that did not mean he did not have PANDAS.

The NIMH staff confirmed that a plasmapheresis blood procedure was not available anywhere in the country for PANDAS patients.

I STARTED A JOURNAL. At our first appointment with Dr. Nicolaides I realized it was not good enough to give her an overview. I needed to be specific. I began recording hour-by-hour entries in a large calendar book that I picked up at Staples. I tracked all of Sammy's medication and behaviors.

My first journal entry was "Didn't leave the room all day." Then:

11:00 a.m.	woke up, 750 mg Augmentin, 2.5 Zyprexa
12:45	up, 30 min compulsions
	hopping, sliding feet, good mood
	very verbal, says he's tired, very chipper
	ate fruit & bowl of raisin bran
2:25	slide to corner/hop back/flap legs
5:00	COMPULSIONS
7:00	4 mg Gabitril
	750 mg Augmentin
	2 hours of COMPULSIONS
	3 meals: fruit & cereal, chicken,
	spaghetti after midnight
1:00 a.m.	bathroom
2:30	sleep

As the days progressed, I realized that nothing could be better than showing Dr. Nicolaides Sammy's behaviors on film. I made a quick trip to Best Buy, but the movie cameras were pricey, and I had one at home. Principal photography would not commence until we got back to Maine.

When we saw Dr. Nicolaides for our next appointment, I had a complete written record. Most important, the entries confirmed that he had improved as the week had progressed. Instead of three or four hours of compulsions a day, he was down to an hour, in spurts that ranged from five to fifteen minutes. He ate a good amount of food and reliably fell asleep by one in the morning. I was still too guarded to be hopeful, but I was relieved that life was clearly a little less painful for him.

Dr. Nicolaides said his tremor was less prominent and that his reflexes were not as brisk. Those kinds of observations were too subtle for me, but I was confident in her judgment. She gave me a plan for medication, told me to keep in close contact, and asked us to come back in four to six weeks. We would need to stay for a week again.

We rested up for a full day at the hotel; then Josh and I packed up the van. Sammy asked to be left alone in the empty room "for five minutes."

Josh and James and I hung around the pool while we waited for Sammy.

After thirty minutes, I stood outside on the patio and carefully peeked into the room through the sliding glass door. He was doing his toy soldier movements. It was a good hour before he left the room and started his trip back through the halls.

Every so often, I sneaked a peek around a corner and reported back to Josh and James on their brother's progress. When he got close to the lobby, the three of us got in the van.

I pulled up to the hotel entrance, and we waited again. Eventually, Sammy—still in the navy polo and bathing suit—shuffled through the lobby door. I slid open his door, waited while he got himself in, and then slid it shut. He made his contorted way to the bench seat at the back and collapsed from exhaustion.

I climbed into the driver's seat, pointed the van north, and we headed home to Maine. Peace started to settle into my psyche. I did not know if Sammy would ever be completely well, but at last we had a doctor who knew what was wrong and how to treat him. I knew that if he was going to get better, it would take a long time.

I had all the time in the world for my son.

14

Cuckoo's Nest

E very month in Maine is special, but August is among the most beautiful.

The air is humid, the water warms up, and everyone is out on the ocean or off at a lake. Flowers bloom in all the gardens. Bradbury's is swamped with summer people heaping their carts full with a week's supplies. My friends go out on their boats and collect lobsters from their traps. If I'm lucky, there are extras for me. I bicycle over to friends' houses and pop in.

In the morning, on a gray day, I wake up listening to the foghorn that blares from Cape Porpoise Harbor. If the sky is clear and the tide is right later that day, I kayak to the lighthouse. I climb the iron stairwell to the very top, gaze off in every direction, and wonder how I got to be so lucky.

At six o'clock, the night is still young, with plenty of light for evening excursions. At seven, the ocean and sky often blend into the exact same shade of white-lit gray. If I am on the ocean, I separate the water from the clouds by the seals that poke their heads up and then gently slide back down again. I like to kayak until that luscious August moon comes up over the ocean and casts a silver path where I float. I sit for a while, soaking it in. It's good luck, just like spotting seals.

After dark, it's fun to roam Kennebunkport. The streets swell with shoppers, while lovers sip wine in crowded restaurants.

This August was different, though. We were still locked in the grip of Sammy's mental illness and didn't know that he stood delicately on the cusp of recovery.

THE DAY AFTER we returned from New Jersey, I called my friend Maureen. Months earlier, I'd said I would come to her son's bar mitzvah. The save-the-date cards, with boats sailing peacefully over the ocean under a brilliant blue sky, had arrived the previous summer. For weeks, I had been giving myself the "you can do it" pep talk, but I knew that I could not. Attending that joyful event—one that I did not think my own son would ever have—would be too much for me to bear. It would take me to an emotionally painful place where I simply could not be.

I was the captain. If I went down, the ship was going with me.

"I can't come to the bar mitzvah." I was weeping.

"It's okay, Beth. I understand," Maureen said.

The first weeks home were a roller coaster. Notations spilled from the pages of my journal in cramped writing that ran off the lines and spread sideways. An arrow next to the date gave me a quick overview of the day: up for good, down for bad, horizontal if he cycled. Boxes, circles, and symbols noted behaviors, medications, and eating habits. I recorded every single thing about his day: when he woke, when he slept, when he did or did not do the compulsive behaviors, the things he said, the things he did, the way he looked at us from the slits of his eyes. I wanted to track exactly how he responded to each medication and to communicate with specificity. "He seemed better on Tuesday" would not be good enough.

He was taking 4 milligrams of Gabitril, 7.5 milligrams of Zyprexa, and 1,500 milligrams of Augmentin each day. Gabitril is a mood stabilizer, sometimes used to treat mania in bipolar disorder. Zyprexa is an antipsychotic that is also used in treating tic disorders, including Tourette's.

If this "medication cocktail" worked as we hoped, Sammy's days would become less emotional, his tics less pronounced, and his behaviors less severe while the Augmentin battled his strep infection. The plan was to gradually eliminate the Gabitril as he stabilized, increase the Zyprexa, and drop him to a maintenance dose of 200 milligrams of Augmentin after three weeks. In the middle of August, I faxed Dr. Nicolaides details about Sammy that indicated that things were somewhat better.

My journal confirmed new patterns. He fell asleep on his couch between nine and ten every night. He woke by ten in the morning. He brushed his teeth for the first time in months. He even made himself take a shower. He cried and yelled to get himself into the shower, but he did it on his own initiative. Whole days went by when he did not need to be left alone for the hours of relentless compulsions. One day, he went outside and walked briefly in the yard.

Josh would be heading back to boarding school soon for his junior year. I was relieved that things were stable enough that I could arrange for a sitter to stay while Josh and I made the long drive north.

Then, two days before our departure, Sammy was back in crisis again. He stopped eating, stopped drinking, and did compulsions on and off all day. He had extreme mood swings: crying and laughing within the space of five minutes. He jabbered and screamed for hours. Even a slight increase in the Zyprexa did not seem to help. I was scrambling again. Sammy was decompensating, and I had to get Josh back to school.

There I was, caught in the emotional tidal wave that comes with being a single mom. I had one son leaving, to whom I desperately wanted to give the right send-off; one son sick and in need of me; and a third potentially getting lost in the mix. With my split heart, I made the decision to try to stay with the plan. I could be back in less than twenty-four hours.

"He's very sick," I told the college-age babysitter over the phone as I brought her up to date. "Do you think you can handle it?"

"It'll be okay," she said. "It's one day. I can do it."

I called Chris and asked, "Are you going to be around? In case it gets even worse."

"I'm here," she said.

Josh's bedroom opened off the den. To pack, we had to carry everything past Sammy. Sammy screamed at us to leave. He raged that he hated us for packing, saying that he needed the peace and quiet more than Josh needed to leave for school. We had to keep stopping and starting. It took twelve hours to pack the van. We finished at midnight.

The babysitter showed up the next morning and reassured me again.

"I'm a psychology major," she said confidently, her ponytail bouncing.

I nodded and gave her Chris's number; then I reviewed the medication instructions and handed her the journal.

"Write everything down," I told her. "Every time he eats or sleeps or twitches. Hour by hour, there should be an entry."

I left with Josh at three that afternoon and drove straight through. Six hours later we checked into a hotel. First thing in the morning, we unpacked his things in his dorm. I gave him a hug, wished him good luck, and raced back to Kennebunkport. All along the way, I called home to check on Sammy.

"It's like he can't stop sneezing" was the first report from the babysitter.

The second time I called, she said, "He keeps babbling, and he yells at me if I ask him what's wrong."

"Don't ask," I instructed. "It makes him worse."

She called when I was still two hours away. "How far away are you?" Sammy was screaming in the background.

"Long time. Does he want to talk to me?" I asked.

"Sammy, do you want to talk to your mother?" I heard her ask. "He's shaking his head, no," she told me, "so I guess not."

"Do you want to call Chris?" I asked.

"I did. She's coming over."

When I finally got back, Sammy was on the couch, under the cushions. All the progress he'd made was gone. The babysitter went home. Chris gave me a hug and left. I collapsed into bed, exhausted and defeated.

What the hell was going on? Why had this medicine stopped working, too?

The next morning, my friend Dianne came to help clean. She found the pills that Sammy had stuffed into the cracks of the couch.

I WATCHED THE PATIENTS do it in *One Flew Over the Cuckoo's Nest.* I knew that some of the children for whom I was guardian *ad litem* "cheeked" their meds. When Sammy—one of the most honest kids ever—pulled this stunt, I recognized that hiding the meds was truly a universal phenomenon of mental illness.

I called Dr. Nicolaides. We reduced all the meds, including the Augmentin, because we no longer had any idea where we were in terms of dosage. Then I talked to Sammy. There was no point in confronting him about hiding the pills.

"Dr. Nicolaides just called," I told him. "She said this is about the time when kids start to hide their pills instead of taking them. She said I have to watch you take every pill and make sure they get swallowed. She makes all the moms do it a few weeks into the program."

Sammy stared at me and said nothing.

"Gotta follow the doctor's orders," I said with a shrug and handed him his pills; then I watched very carefully as he swallowed each one.

It had been about a month since we'd seen Dr. Nicolaides. Sammy was back in crisis every day. The wailing, howling, and screaming were all back. I held it together as best I could. I told myself we had been sidelined and would find our way back to recovery.

"Tell her the strep is coming back!" he shrieked from the bathroom in the middle of sobs one morning. "It was getting better, but it's getting harder and harder to get around."

There was a pounding noise coming from the bathroom. I hoped it was not his head.

"Tell her I'm having a weird twitching thing! Sometimes my whole body will start shaking uncontrollably, or I'll suddenly scream out and I don't know why!" he cried. "Tell her my knees hurt!"

I called Dr. Nicolaides. I assured her that I had watched him take every pill, every day. She said to wait four more days. If he had not improved, I should up the Augmentin or the Zyprexa at my discretion. Day 4 was going to fall on the weekend, so I would make the decision on my own.

Sammy got worse. For the next four days he screamed, howled, and sobbed. He begged me to take the den door off its hinges so that he could move around more easily. When I came back with the screwdriver, he cried and screamed for me to leave the door alone. He held his ears shut and jabbered relentlessly. He had verbal tics and constantly cleared his throat.

"I hate this!!! I hate this!!!" Sammy screamed while he stood in the den, dripping with sweat from the physical exertion of all the behaviors. It was the morning of the fourth day.

He huffed and puffed, rubbed his feet on the carpet, held his ears shut, gasped for breath, hopped, and pounded, over and over again. After two and a half hours of watching, I wanted to rip my hair from my skull. He was in too much pain to wait any longer. It could go either way, but I had to do something. I decided to increase the Augmentin. I would put it back up to 1,500 milligrams a day.

He had already taken 250 milligrams of Augmentin. So at ten-thirty that morning, I gave him another 500 milligrams. Within two hours, all the compulsions had stopped, and he ate a full lunch. After lunch, he played a board game. In the early afternoon, he gasped and shivered as if he were having an anxiety attack, but at three P.M., he came upstairs briefly and asked for a snack. He took his pills dutifully at five, including another 750 milligrams of Augmentin. He had pizza for dinner and drifted off to sleep on his couch at seven-fifteen.

For five days, Sammy remained at 1,500 milligrams of Augmentin. He did not have a single emotional breakdown for those five days. The compulsive behaviors continued but were less severe, never to the point that he broke out in a sweat. He ate regular meals. He was asleep by eight each night and woke at about eight each morning. His tutor Ruth came, and he participated. His verbal tics faded and finally disappeared. He smiled.

I called Dr. Nicolaides and told her what was going on. I also repeated what Sammy had said about the strep coming back.

"How much higher can we take the Augmentin?" I pressed.

"If we go with extended release, it's called Augmentin XR, we can go as high as two thousand milligrams a day," she answered.

"Let's do it," I said without hesitating.

And each day he got better.

DOCTORS ARE CAUTIOUS ABOUT overmedicating with antibiotics because of the risks the drugs can pose. There are risks of developing resistance. There are risks to the bowels because antibiotics kill off the good bacteria as well as the bad. I was fully willing to take on those risks because I knew what I had on my hands in the absence of the Augmentin. I also knew from Dr. Moore that standard treatment for rheumatic fever had been penicillin, sometimes for as long as twenty years. Those patients did well. Maybe long-term antibiotic treatment was what Sammy needed.

"Have him eat yogurt and get him Culturelle," my ex-brother-in-law the doctor told me.

"Get him what?"

"Culturelle. It's a probiotic, in a capsule; it's sold over the counter. Give him one every day."

"Morning or afternoon?" I asked.

"Midday, right between the doses of antibiotics. It's more effective that way."

Yogurt and Culturelle could help replace the good bacteria. Blood work could track how his bowels were doing through a blood test called a CBC (complete blood count) with differential.

Sammy took his first pills as soon as he woke up. By four P.M. he would be asking for the evening dose. It reminded me of the way I needed painkillers after my C-sections. Compulsive behaviors still dominated his days, and when he moved he was stiff, but the crisis episodes faded completely over September. One day, when he had forced himself into the shower, I heard the wail and braced myself for the scream. It turned into a tune. He was singing.

In addition to recording everything in my journal, I surreptitiously videotaped Sammy's behaviors. He did not want me to take any pictures of him, but I felt that the information was vital. I wanted Dr. Nicolaides to see what the behaviors looked like, not just hear about them from me. So I poked the camera around a doorway or placed it on a shelf. For his occasional trips outside, I pointed it through a window. He was usually so focused on his latest kick, twist, and chop that he did not notice as long as I kept quiet. Once in a while, he caught me.

One morning, I was filming him in the yard, from the second floor. He suddenly looked up and noticed the camera sticking out the window. I quickly swung it over toward the swing set.

"Heeeeeeey, what are you doing?" he called.

"James needs this for school." I kept the camera trained on the swing set. "They're studying something, and he needs a movie of the swing set."

"Why would he need a movie of the swing set?" Sammy asked skeptically.

"Sammy, I don't know." I acted irritated. "I just do what my children tell me. There, I'm done." I pulled the camera back and snapped the window shut.

Another time, when I heard him coming upstairs, I set the camera up in a kitchen cabinet. I pushed it in between all the cereal boxes and aimed it toward the center of the room. Sammy hopped, swirled, and shuffled his way over the invisible walls and past the cabinet. In the middle of a particularly gymnastic compulsion—a cross between a slow-motion karate kick and an ambitious rabbit hop—his head turned to the side. He caught sight of the tiny red light on the camera.

"What's that?" He asked, frozen in mid-motion, his leg hanging in the air.

"What?" I feigned nonchalance.

"There's a red light in the cereal cabinet."

I walked over and looked. "Oh that? My cell phone's charging up in there." I slammed the cabinet door shut and calmly loaded dishes into the dishwasher, hoping like heck he wouldn't ask a follow-up.

Sammy paused for a moment, peering under his arm, then swung his leg around and continued on his way.

Ruth came every day to tutor. Sammy lay on his couch, expressionless, and she read to him. He was flat on his stomach or back, his free arm extended and stretched toward the floor.

During the two hours when Ruth tutored, I attended meetings, made court appearances, and visited children on my caseload. On Mondays, I could be out for a long stretch because Dianne came to clean. Sammy related easily to her. With Dianne at the house for three or four hours and Ruth there for another two, I had a good five- or six-hour stretch available to work. Mondays were liberating.

The real work continued to take place late at night, when I researched online. I wanted definitive information on PANDAS. This was impossible, though, because—unlike with the law—there is no central depository of medical information. A legal question can be researched in an orderly fashion up through the courts to figure out the current state of the law. Medical information is all over the place. You might find the answer, you might not, or you might stumble across it by chance.

Although Sammy was doing better, it was tentative, and Dr. Nicolaides encouraged me to keep all our options open. If things got desperate again, he might need a blood procedure. Since plasmapheresis was not available, the only choice would be to try to dilute the level of strep antibodies in his bloodstream by introducing a pooled blood product through an IV

Ig. This idea did not sit well with me. Tainted blood had once infected patients with HIV. What undiscovered culprit might be next? Nonetheless, I continued to explore.

In order to get an IV Ig, I was back to needing a pediatric neurologist. There was only one in the entire state of Maine. I faxed him Sammy's history. His nurse called to say he did not have the appropriate expertise to treat Sammy. I began my second round of faxes, telephone calls, and e-mails to Boston. Eventually, I set up appointments for Sammy at two hospitals: one at Children's Hospital and the other at a place with an odd name, the Floating Hospital. At Children's Hospital, the earliest appointment I could get was for the last week in October. The Floating Hospital booked us for January. He was waitlisted at both in case something became available earlier.

Sammy remained at 2,000 milligrams of Augmentin XR each day. The Zyprexa was up to 12.5 milligrams. The plan remained to eliminate the Gabitril once we were confident that he was responding to the higher dose of Zyprexa.

One of the side effects of Zyprexa is weight gain. And with Sammy, this effect was obvious. I had not experienced anyone consuming food like Sammy. He developed a penchant for garlic toast, and I served it by the loaf. In one day, he would eat cereal and fruit to start, one or two whole watermelons, two loaves of garlic bread, a chicken leg, rice, a couple of bowls of chicken soup, boxes of blueberries, bowls of strawberries, and often two servings of spaghetti and meatballs. I was happily running up and down the stairs with plates and bowls loaded up with his latest requests.

"MOM!" His voice blared through on the walkie-talkie. I always jumped when it burst boldly into what I now considered my medical research station. I wrote down his most recent menu request. After "Over and out," I whipped up his order and delivered it to him at his outpost in the den. The food had to be served on the light-colored (not the dark-colored) television table, with the silver-handled (not the black-handled) fork and knife. Sometimes, when he forgot something and had to radio me again, he'd have tears in his eyes when I arrived. He felt bad about being helpless and my waiting on him hand and foot.

"Now, Sammy, don't you worry about that. You just tell me what you need." I wished I could give him a hug.

WE WENT BACK to see Dr. Nicolaides six weeks after our first visit. There was no question that Sammy was doing better. He was no longer dehydrated. When we went in for updated blood work, the red stuff gushed willingly into the tubes. His strep titer had dropped to 200.

During the week before we left for New Jersey, he came upstairs twice: one time to change out of the bathing suit he'd put on in July, and the other time to take a shower. His teeth were dirty and he would not use soap, so his hair was matted with grease, but the shower was still a huge step. There were whole days that had passed without any compulsions. On the morning of our departure, it took him only five minutes to get from the house to the van.

Josh was in boarding school, but James was with us. He spent a good part of the long ride to the Doubletree lobbying for Sammy's chocolate chip cookie.

"They're my walkie-talkies, and I let you use them," James finally pointed out.

"Fine, James. Have the cookie. I don't want it anyway."
Sammy was spread out across the third seat in the back.

We drove on in silence for a while as James basked in his
victory, until . . .

"What if they give you more than one?"

"Mom gets it," answered Sammy.

"Mom?" James asked.

"I'm okay with you having it," I answered.

"It's my cookie, I'll decide," said Sammy.

"Sorry," I said.

The ordinariness of this sibling banter was reassuring. It felt
normal.

AT THE DOUBLETREE, it took Sammy only thirty minutes to
get from the lobby to our first-floor room. He was dripping
with sweat from all the jumping and twisting, but compared to
our last trip, his speed was astonishing. I filmed him through
hall windows while he snaked his way down the hall.

When he reached the room, he went immediately into the
bathroom and began singing as he took a shower. After that,
he put on a bathing suit and headed for the pool. Soon, both
he and James were going back and forth between the pool and
the Jacuzzi. I sat poolside and let myself feel like any other parent watching my children have fun.

The next morning, we saw Dr. Nicolaides. Between the
footage, my journal, and the faxes, she had a complete description of Sammy's daily world. Or as complete as I could make
it for her, as Sammy wasn't talking much about these issues. I
was worried about the amount of food Sammy consumed. He
gained pounds every week, and the *New York Times* had recently

reported a possible link between Zyprexa and diabetes. She felt the Zyprexa was essential, and that we could monitor the diabetes risk through regular blood work. The weight gain was something we would deal with later.

Based on his progress, she felt it was time to eliminate the Gabitril. She instructed us to maintain the Augmentin and Zyprexa. We went back to the hotel to wait the five days until our next appointment. There was a discernible difference in Sammy over the next five days without the Gabitril. All of his movements became stiffer. He jabbered more than usual. He cleared his throat a lot and added a new verbal tic, a "hmmm" in the middle of sentences. However, there was progress, too. He brushed his teeth. He asked to go to the mall. Once there, he moved in the shape of an upside-down L, jumped every pattern, and backtracked incessantly—but he was at the mall!

At our appointment, Dr. Nicolaides reduced the Zyprexa to 10 milligrams and asked us to come back in a month.

"Don't you think you should try to find someone closer to home?" she asked, handing me a prescription for updated blood work.

"We won't stop coming to see you, but if you know someone, I'm willing to see that doctor, too."

"Dan Geller," she said, "in Boston."

SEPTEMBER DREW TO a glorious close. One Saturday morning, Sammy came upstairs, sat down at the table, and asked for pancakes.

"How do you want them, baby?" I tried not to shout with glee as I clattered about the kitchen, pulling out pans and mix and eggs. "Plain, blueberries, chocolate chips, do you want syrup or butter or what?"

It had been so long since Sammy had eaten pancakes that I could not remember how he liked them. The noise in the kitchen woke up James. He came out from his bedroom wearing his favorite frog-print pajamas.

"You woke me up." He sat down at the table and rubbed the sleep dust from his eyes.

"I'm sorry, sweetie. I was just so excited. Sammy asked for pancakes!"

"Is that good?" He yawned.

"Well, yes, it is. It's been a long time since Sammy sat and ate pancakes."

James looked at Sammy. "Maybe you won't eat them again because of the excessive-compulsion disorder."

"This isn't permanent, James. This is a nonpermanent mental condition," Sammy said definitively.

From your lips to God's ears, I thought, and for that moment, on that splendid September morning, I let my heart believe him.

15

Irresistible Prejudice

The leaf peepers come in October. The trees explode in gold and orange and red, and Kennebunkport explodes in controversy over the buses that bring the peepers.

I have never really followed the bus controversy, but I did get a bit interested one year when a busload of peepers almost ran me over accidentally. I was on my road bike, racing along Ocean Avenue past Walker's Point, when the bus suddenly accelerated, and I was forced to the side of the road.

October is also the month when our local mice try to move into our houses. While my friends and I are thinking about winter clothes and wondering if the kids will fit into last year's jackets, the mice are searching for a warm winter place to call home. As we drive to one another's houses to drop off snow pants and jackets that might fit the younger ones, the mice diligently try to sneak their way into the walls.

In the October of Sammy's recovery, I managed to take a few bike rides and kayaked around the cove for one quick, blessed trip. But keeping track of what was going on with Sammy was still my only avocation. My friends had been bugging me for months to go out for my birthday. I finally agreed that I would feel comfortable leaving Sammy for a few hours, but only if we had breakfast at the coffee shop right up the street. Seated at the table next to us were some movie people who had just finished shooting *Empire Falls* for HBO. Paul Newman had a starring role, and Bradbury's had a big poster in its window advertising itself as the local distributor of Newman's Own salad dressing.

My belated birthday breakfast was the longest period of time that I had been with my friends in sixteen months.

WHEN I BEGAN MY Sammy journal, the arrows pointing up for good days were few and far between. Two months later, things were very different. There were long stretches of good days followed by a dip for a day or two. At first, a bad day caused me grave concern. Was it a permanent slide? Why was he suddenly failing? But studying my journal let me see a pattern. Sammy was recovering in waves. With that information, I was no longer rattled by the bad days. I knew the good days would be back.

On the good days, he came upstairs every so often to request a meal or perhaps "the usual." I knew he'd be upstairs shortly when I'd hear him open the cabinet door at the base of the stairs. It meant he was ducking his head into the cabinet to take a breath, and that I'd soon hear his footsteps rushing upstairs. It was a sound that delighted me.

On the bad days, I told him with confidence, "It will get better."

Sometimes the dips were triggered. Once, James accidentally touched Sammy's arm and sent him into a storm of screams and compulsions. Other times, it came out of the blue. He might wake feeling depressed or say he felt frustrated. I comforted myself during these low periods by studying the patterns in my journal. He'd been up and down before; he'd be up and down again. Overall, the picture was positive. He reliably fell asleep by eight in the evening. My anxiety lessened, and I woke up only two or three times a night. Life had started to have a reliable ebb and flow.

On the morning of October 4, my journal reflected eleven up days in a row. I was hoping for another good day. Sammy was on his couch when I handed him the small glass he used for water and the pink pottery bowl that held his pills. This had become our standard morning routine after he walkie-talkied to say he was awake.

"How are you feeling this morning?" I asked my usual question after he took the last pill.

"Good, Mom." He yawned.

"Garlic toast and soup for breakfast?"

Sammy nodded yes. I turned to go get the food.

"Hey, Mom?"

I turned back, wondering what he'd forgotten.

"I really do think this is temporary." He was smiling.

My eyes welled up as I sucked in a long, deep breath.

"You're going to cry, aren't you, Mom?"

"Probably," I sniffled, then nearly floated upstairs to get his food.

CHRIS CALLED ONE AFTERNOON to find out if she could bring Devers over. He hadn't seen Sammy for a while, and he wanted to visit. I thought Sammy was well enough for them to watch television together, and I was just about to say yes, when I had a thought.

"What's he got on his feet?" I asked.

"Devers?"

"Yup."

"I don't know. Let me look." There was a brief moment while Chris went searching for Devers; then she came back on the phone and said, "Sandals."

"No sandals—or if he wants to wear sandals, he has to wear socks," I said.

"Can he wear sneakers?" she asked.

"Sneakers are okay, but wait—he better wear socks with the sneakers in case he takes the sneakers off. We gotta be careful about bare feet; sends Sammy right over the edge."

There was a beat before we dissolved into uncontrollable giggles. It felt good to laugh like that again.

I had recently learned from Sammy that we had to keep our feet covered because bare feet triggered a round of compulsions. Sammy had become comfortable enough to begin to fill us in on bits and pieces of what went on inside his head. Bare feet had been the reason he'd kept his eyes shut tight on the day we had moved. We'd been in sandals, and he could not stand the sight of toes.

JOSH CAME HOME for a weekend. With the three of them around, the action in the kitchen was nonstop. An entire refrigerator's worth of food often disappeared in less than a day, although they could never seem to find anything to eat. I used to be frustrated by this; but then I'd decided to think of it as endearing.

Even at a young age, any one of the three fruits of my womb would stand in front of the open refrigerator door, with the juice carton almost toppling from the shelf onto his head, and call out the same thing:

"Mom, where's the juice?"

"It's in there," I'd call back. A moment would pass.

"Can't find it."

"I know it's there," I'd call back, trying to stay positive.

"I think we're out, Mom."

Then I'd stop whatever I was doing, go to the refrigerator, and find it in two and a half seconds. The same procedure occurred with missing shoes, backpacks, and books.

I was especially glad Josh was home for that extended weekend because I was sick to death of emptying mousetraps. I knew he would empty some for me. My house was overrun with mice. I had bigger things on my mind than trapping a few mice, so I had ignored their leaping and jumping and rolling until two ran busily through my office one sunny afternoon. I was on the phone with my friend Justine, discussing a case, when the mice tumbled by.

JUSTINE AND I MET when she was assigned as Maine's assistant attorney general on some of my child protection cases. I had seen her name on paperwork before we'd been introduced.

One day at the courthouse, I'd asked my attorney friend

Glenda, "Who's Justine, the new AAG? I have to give her a copy of my guardian *ad litem* report."

"She was just here, but now I don't see her," said Glenda, glancing around the courthouse lobby, which was crowded with lawyers and clients. "You'll spot her, though. She looks like an airline stewardess, and I mean that in a good way."

Shortly thereafter, I noticed a tall, elegant woman in a navy blue suit with her hair in a French twist. Her back was toward me.

I walked up and said, "Justine?"

"Yes?" She turned, and I saw that she was about five months pregnant. I later learned that this would be her second child.

A few months later, she was teary-eyed one morning at the courthouse.

"I don't see how I can handle this job and be a good mom," she told me.

"Become a guardian *ad litem* like me," I said. "It will change your life."

And that's just what she did. Now we often talked over cases when we ran into complicated problems.

"TWO MICE JUST RAN BY," I said to Justine in the middle of our phone conversation. "They're all over the house. I've got to get rid of them."

"The only kind way to kill mice is with traps," she said.

I went out and bought every mouse contraption I could find, including sonic buzzers that plugged into outlets. The buzzers seemed useless, but every morning there were tails sticking out of the traps. I'd bought the box style so that I did not actually have to see the dead mouse, just its tail. I walked into the woods with a full trap, turned my head, opened the top, lifted the bar, and made a face when the dead mouse hit the ground with a little *thunk*.

On this particular weekend, in the middle of mouse mania, not only was Josh home but Devers was over. We were all in our socks. The boys, including James, were at the table getting ready to play Dungeons & Dragons. The table was covered with lined sheets of paper on which they wrote traits and features to build characters. There were open books with titles like *Player's Handbook, Monster Manual,* and *Dungeon Master's Guide.* I stood in the kitchen, making spaghetti sauce. Suddenly, I spotted a mouse.

Uh-oh, I thought as I tapped some Parmesan into the sauce, *here comes trouble.*

The mouse was behind Sammy's back, moving slowly across the floor. I watched it make its way along the floorboard, then stop directly behind Sammy. I had not come across research detailing the effect mice have on compulsions, but I knew it could not be good.

Just then, Sammy stood up.

"I've got to go to the bathroom," he announced and hopped off, quick as a bunny. Luckily, he did not notice the mouse.

"Help," I said in a frantic whisper the minute he shut the bathroom door. "There's a mouse . . ." I pointed. "We can't let Sammy see it!"

We all scurried around, trying to figure out what to do with the mouse. Devers came up with an empty box just as we heard Sammy fiddling with the handle to open the bathroom door. I popped the box over the mouse, and we all raced back to our places. The boys grabbed their seats and studied their books. I calmly added garlic powder to the sauce and stirred. Sammy hopped out of the bathroom, over to the table, and sat down, oblivious. After lunch, when they were all downstairs, I lifted the box with trepidation. The mouse was dead.

WHEN WE WENT BACK to see Dr. Nicolaides a few weeks later, we were full of positive news. And this time, Sammy beat me to the hotel room. Although he remained riddled with compulsions, he had not been in crisis since early September. He was working well with the tutor. We'd removed his braces because he could not brush his teeth. He'd tolerated that well, along with a subsequent cleaning at the dentist's office.

Dr. Nicolaides and I reviewed my journal notes and my new tapes. We agreed to lower the Augmentin XR from 2,000 milligrams to 1,000. The Zyprexa would remain at 10 milligrams. She felt comfortable with his progress and sent us home the next day.

A few days later, when I came back from the pharmacy, James was excited.

"Dad called. He said he's coming from California for a visit," James said happily.

"Terrific," I answered.

"He said he'll take us to the mall, too."

"That'll be fun," I said aloud, silently wondering if Sammy could handle a trip to the mall.

The boys spent most of Saturday with their dad in my yard, building a bonfire and roasting marshmallows. They planned a trip to the mall for Sunday. I had my doubts, but Sammy woke up determined, so off they went. Sammy had a tough time at the mall; but he did not have a crisis, and he came home with a brand-new notebook computer. Purchasing that notebook turned out to be a great decision. It eventually opened up Sammy's world the way my Bondi blue iMac had granted me access to the heart of PANDAS research.

For now, though, his world stayed small.

On Monday, Sammy woke up screaming and crying. It had been six weeks since his last such meltdown. I told him it was understandable because of all the action. He had just finished a trip to New Jersey, a visit with his dad, and a long day at the mall.

"It'll be okay," I assured him.

I was wrong. Over the next two weeks, Sammy spiraled downward. Crises were interspersed with days that went smoothly. I was disappointed, but there was a part of me that simply accepted it.

"I'm not sure I ever really believed he would maintain," I told my mom sadly when she called for an update. "But we've had a busy time, so I'm hopeful that's it: New Jersey last week and then his dad's visit. Maybe he's anxious about the doctor appointments we've got coming up in Boston. We're seeing a neurologist at Children's Hospital and also a child psychiatrist named Dan Geller."

OUR VISIT AT Children's Hospital was with one of the top pediatric neurologists in Boston. I gave him Sammy's history and said that although he was much improved from his low point three months earlier, he was on a downward spiral again.

As the neurologist examined Sammy, he informed me that there could not be a diagnosis of PANDAS unless blood tests revealed elevated antineuronal antibodies.

"This is new information for me." I was perplexed. "I've spoken with NIMH, with Dr. Tanya Murphy in Florida, and, of course, Dr. Nicolaides. We've run all kinds of blood tests, but no one's ever mentioned antineuronal antibodies."

"Well, you can't have PANDAS if the antineuronal antibodies aren't elevated," he said curtly.

"Why wouldn't NIMH know this? They said they've spoken with me 'more than any other parent.' Why wouldn't they have mentioned it?" I mused, genuinely puzzled, and then added, "Maybe there's a difference of opinion over the significance of these antibodies?"

He gave me the you're-not-a-doctor-and-have-absolutely-no-idea-what-you're-talking-about look (which did not faze me) and said—definitively—that without them, Sammy had Tourette syndrome. Instead of calling it Tourette's, though, he kept calling it "Gilles de la Tourette syndrome," with a fancy French accent. I was not impressed.

The exam itself went relatively well, except when the doctor wanted Sammy to close his eyes and touch his nose. Sammy almost burst into tears. As best I understood it, once Sammy closed his eyes he could not open them again until the morning.

I was not fond of how the doctor handled the whole thing, but Sammy finally managed. There followed a lot of touching-the-nose-with-the-fingertip type of exercises. The neurologist was confident that Sammy had not suffered any brain damage and that he did not need a brain scan. We left with an order for blood work, which, when completed, did not reveal the presence of elevated antineuronal antibodies. The neurologist mailed me a report stating that, in his opinion, Sammy did not have PANDAS but did have Tourette's.

To this day, I have not found anyone else who holds the opinion that antineuronal antibodies are a necessary component of a diagnosis of PANDAS.

OUR APPOINTMENT WITH Dr. Daniel Geller was scheduled for the last day of October. Sammy had a fifteen-minute meltdown just before we left: hyperventilating, pounding, and yelping.

Dr. Geller and Dr. Nicolaides had done their training together as developmental pediatricians at Johns Hopkins. After that, Dr. Geller went on to study psychiatry. He is considered one of the top five child psychiatrists in the country for certain disorders, including OCD. He is a faculty member at Harvard Medical School. He directs the pediatric OCD program at Massachusetts General Hospital. He is known all over the world. When you mention Dr. Geller's name to doctors or researchers in the field, they say, "Do you mean *the* Dan Geller?"

Two weeks before our appointment, I mailed Dr. Geller a detailed letter to give him an overview of Sammy's condition. I was always concerned that I would forget information during doctor visits, so composing a written record in advance was for me—as well as the doctor—the best way to go. It also alleviated the need to go over it all in front of Sammy. I thought that might be painful for him. In the letter, I explained Sammy's rituals and the things he avoided. I wrote about the five morning drinks that made up "the usual," and the invisible walls over which he stepped. I mentioned how he held his breath when he came upstairs, that he preferred to urinate outside, and his preference for green and khaki clothes. I covered his heightened sense of touch and his aversion to bare feet. I also

p.

and the atmos-
he air had been
w calmness set-
became an ob-
ety meter drop
ocean blue of
or a minute or

"there are lots

mediate com-

all these chil-

d Dr. Geller.
his list are the

a look at this
.

come closer.

behind Dr.
d Sammy's

backward
ting room,

edications from his

Geller sat behind his
t. I sat in one of the
of the big, friendly
dows. Sammy, in his
nd paced. He looked
of his eyes. Everything
to escape—particularly
the doors. Dr. Geller

erald wrote that Gatsby
ejudice in your favor";
s you wanted to be un-
d like to believe in your-
impression of you that, at
is was the way Dr. Geller

d Australian accent, as he
ed a yellow highlighter to
st important points. Occa-
perwork to ask a question.
and things you like to do?"

d.

papers and kept highlighting.
h written detail. I had also sent
od tests. As he scanned them,
ntibody theory past him.

"I think it's PANDAS," he said, looking u

Then Dr. Geller leaned back in his chair,
phere in the room began to shift. Until then,
charged with the static of Sammy's anxiety. N
tled into the room as the doctor gazed at him.
server, watching the needle on Sammy's anxi
slowly from the bright red of "danger" to the
"peace." Dr. Geller watched Sammy intently
two, and then he spoke.

"Now you know, Sammy," he said gently,
and lots of children like you . . ."

Sammy cocked his head slightly, finding im
fort in these words he had not heard before.

". . . and I have a list here of the things that
dren have told me bother them."

Sammy turned his left ear inquisitively towa

"I'm just wondering if any of the things on t
kinds of things that bother you."

Sammy widened the slits of his eyes just a bit.

"I wonder if you would come here and take
list with me?" Dr. Geller beckoned with his hand

Sammy stayed put.

"Here." Dr. Geller gestured again for him to
Sammy turned to face Dr. Geller.

"Will you?" Dr. Geller beckoned again.

Sammy, wary but intrigued, shuffled over, stood
Geller, and read the list over his shoulder. I watch
body relax as they talked about the list.

When the appointment was over, Sammy exite
through the door that led to Dr. Geller's tiny wai

and then he circled around to the street. I met him outside, and we headed for the van.

On the way back to Maine, Sammy sat quietly in the seat behind me. It was the first time he had sat in that seat in over a year. After a bit, he asked if we could stop at a restaurant for lunch. I found a Friendly's, pulled in, and parked. I slid the van door open for him. He swirled and jerked his way through the parking lot to the restaurant.

"Sorry, sorry," he offered as he accidentally tromped over a few customers' feet on the way to our booth.

Then we sat and ate like any mother and son might do. Except that I was thinking about the miracle of sharing a meal in a public place with my son and, even more, about the miracle of brilliant doctors.

In Dan Geller, we'd found a doctor who understood my son's heart.

16

The Nonbelievers

Doctors are scientists. They like to rely on studies. The problem is, some doctors get so invested in their positions that they have a hard time when a different truth stares them right in the face. Especially if that truth can be dismissed as "anecdotal."

Take the doctor who told me, "Even after hearing Sammy's story, if a child walked in the door tomorrow presenting with those behaviors, I would not run a strep test."

"Why not?" I tried not to throttle her as I took back my copy of the *Boston Globe* article and the research I had handed her.

"Because I don't believe it." She shrugged.

"Let me get this straight," I said carefully, trying to restrain myself. "My family just went through hell for over a year. My kid locked himself in bathrooms and screamed for hours. I had over ten thousand dollars in medical expenses for him, and you

would not run a blood test to figure out if strep might possibly
be what's wrong?"

"That's right," she said.

She used to be one of my doctors. I left her practice that day.

The PANDAS nonbelievers are a committed group. They
say memorable things in important places—for example, in the
New York Times Magazine. On May 22, 2005, it ran an article
that discussed the link between strep and children with rapid-
onset OCD. Dr. Roger Kurlan, the leading nonbeliever, was
quoted as saying, "In the prior two weeks, 90 percent of these
kids might also have eaten pizza. Can I make an association
that pizza is linked to OCD?"

He might be on to something, but I don't think so.

Particularly given a compelling study from researchers at the
Institute of Neurology in London entitled "Tourette's Syndrome: A Cross Sectional Study to Examine the PANDAS Hypothesis." One hundred patients with Tourette's were studied,
along with a control group.

In plain English, the study found that the strep titer was
raised in 64 percent of children with Tourette's and in 68 percent of the adults, compared with an average of 12 percent of
the control group. It's conceivable that 90 percent of the children ate pizza by chance, but a chance connection between elevated titers in this many children with Tourette's seems unlikely.
In fact, statistically, there is less than a one in ten thousand
chance that this is a coincidence.

While I am not sincerely puzzling over the pizza link, I am
concerned about whether a significant portion of the population may be struggling with a mental illness that has its root
cause in an infection.

AS WE MOVED INTO November, Sammy made gains but also fell apart. Since both things were happening at the same time, it was hard to make an assessment. On the plus side, he participated more with the tutor and answered the telephone when I was out.

"HELLO!" he'd blare, holding the receiver about two inches from his ear, with a tissue operating as a protective barrier for his palm.

"IS YOUR MOM THERE?" the caller would shout back.

Yet there was an increase in the number of emotional breakdowns when he would suddenly burst into tears. The first lasted five minutes and happened two weeks after we lowered the dose of Augmentin. Soon they came every other day as full-blown meltdowns: crying, screaming, hyperventilating, and yelping. His movements became stiffer. He looked bloated and gray. We ran another blood test. It had been twenty-six days since we had lowered the Augmentin, and his strep titer was back up to 400. Dr. Nicolaides doubled the Augmentin to 2,000 milligrams again. After that, it was four months before he had another breakdown.

Sammy did not know about the change in dosage. He simply took the pills I handed him. I kept quiet because I wanted to know if the medicine was working without the variable of his reacting to information about the dosage. I did not know it at the time, but I was running my own single-subject reversal design. B. F. Skinner popularized this model when he studied learning in individual animals. He made repeated observations during the baseline, followed by a treatment period, followed by a return to the baseline. By observing and recording Sammy's behaviors during periods of different doses of Augmentin, I unknowingly followed B. F. Skinner's lead.

Doubling the dose of Augmentin XR had a remarkable effect. On the second day of the doubled dose, he had no emotional breakdown. On the third day, he was less stiff. On the fourth day, Chris visited and said he looked "clearly better—something about the eyes."

On the seventh day, Sammy said, "Mom, I'm going to spend the rest of the winter upstairs." He began sleeping in his room.

He soon completed his first successful school assignment of the year, a short story using primarily one-syllable words. He dictated the story to the tutor while he paced across the cushions of the couches in the den.

> *Once upon a time there was a strange boy who liked to do strange things. Though all his friends mocked him for his strange acts, none could stop the boy from his strange play.*
>
> *The next day at school he met a girl who did silly acts, and soon the strange boy had a strange thought with him and the silly girl.*
>
> *And though he did not know it, the silly girl had the same thoughts as the strange boy. So one day the strange boy had to ask the silly girl if she had the same thoughts as he did.*
>
> *When the girl said yes, it was true love.*
>
> *The End*

SAMMY WAS BACK in counseling with his local psychologist and able to attend on a regular basis. He needed help to break the behavior patterns that had become habits. He and the psychologist talked about tackling one problem behavior at a time and trying to conquer it. Sammy was ready and able to work. His first task was to concentrate on walking without the swirls and high steps that dominated his movements.

In mid-November, we went to see Dr. Nicolaides. She came to the reception area, and we greeted her with big smiles.

"Sammy, show her how you can walk," I said proudly.

"I can do it like this," he said as he walked flat-footed across the room. "It just *feels* better to do it like this," he said, adding a swirl and a high step.

Dr. Nicolaides and I reviewed my journal notes and recent videotapes. She said she had been experiencing success with a relatively new medicine called Strattera. She thought it might help. We agreed to add the Strattera over Thanksgiving break, because Sammy would be on vacation from his schoolwork. The Augmentin and Zyprexa would not change. When adjusting medication, it is helpful to have as few variables as possible so that the effect—positive or negative—can be accurately assessed. For the four days of Thanksgiving weekend, the house would be quiet. There would be no tutoring or school assignments, and Josh and James would be going to their paternal grandmother's in New York. Any reaction Sammy might have would clearly be due to the new medicine.

He started with 25 milligrams of the Strattera on Thanksgiving morning. For the first Thanksgiving that Sammy was sick, I could not leave the house. For this one, I would go to

Tracy's and share it with her brood, but I'd keep it short because Sammy would be home alone.

"You're sure you'll be okay?" I stood at the door, ready to
leave, holding my keys and the large salad I was bringing. I'd
added avocado and sprouts because most of my friends in
Maine thought that was exotic.

"Mom, I'll be *fine*," he assured me from the couch. That
got me uptight.

Six months earlier, when Sammy was desperately ill, he'd
sneered at me, "I'm *fine*, Mom. Even if I was lying in a hospital bed, stabbed and bleeding, I would still say I was fine."

I had to admit, he did seem fine. He was not in a hospital
bed but, rather, watching television comfortably at home, so
I darted out the door.

At Tracy's, I gobbled turkey and observed, "So you like
this American holiday?"

"The English were there for the first one," she reminded me.

I rushed home to Sammy right after tea. As I walked in the
front door, the telephone rang. Sammy stood up from his
couch, picked it up, and said hello.

"It's Josh." Sammy handed the telephone to me.

I took it from him, somewhat stunned. He had pressed it to
his ear. He had not shouted, and no tissue had operated as a
safety barrier.

On the Sunday after Thanksgiving, Sammy went to Devers's
house to visit. I called Chris after an hour to check in.

"Is he doing okay?"

"Better than okay. He and Devers are outside chasing the
dog around."

"Oh my goodness!"

Sammy was positively giddy when he got home. That night, he took a bath and worked hard at brushing his teeth. When he climbed into bed with a book to read, then flicked the switch of his reading lamp, it felt like old times. I bit my lip and recorded this milestone in my journal, wondering if I might jinx it by writing it down.

A few days later, we were at the oral surgeon's. Sammy had to have a tooth removed. Because the tooth was growing sideways, it was impossible to delay the extraction any longer. I coordinated communication between the oral surgeon and Dr. Nicolaides to make sure there was no conflict between the painkillers and the psychotropic medication. Sammy was comfortable with the impending procedure, but I was a nervous wreck. I was scared he might have an adverse reaction that would trigger all the compulsions again. Afterward, he took two Tylenol and was fine.

The next day Sammy was upstairs, sipping soup for breakfast, when he jumped up and rushed into the bathroom. On his way back, I heard a whooshing sound. Was that really the toilet? Who knew that the sound of a flushing toilet could become so beautiful? Ten days after Thanksgiving, Sammy let me cut his hair. I did my best to scissor through the greasy locks, then used clippers to shear away the overgrowth. Afterward, Sammy stood in front of the bathroom mirror and turned his head from side to side, checking out the cut.

"Know what, Mom? I think I need to use shampoo." Five minutes later, he was in the shower, scrubbing up.

The gains were coming at the same breathless pace as the compulsive behaviors that once took over his life. Strattera had to be the explanation for this remarkable progress. Augmentin managed the infection. Strattera let him break down the psychological barriers that held him back.

The children's paternal aunt Leah called the next week. She said she'd loved seeing Josh and James at Thanksgiving, but she'd missed Sammy and me. She was having an eightieth birthday party for her mom in February, in New York City. She asked me to put it on our calendar just in case Sammy was well enough.

I was hopeful but realistic. "We'll try," I said, "but we probably won't make it."

WE ALTERNATED APPOINTMENTS BETWEEN Dr. Nicolaides and Dr. Geller so that Sammy saw one of them each month. Our mid-December appointment with Dr. Geller was full of energy. We discussed the recent addition of Strattera and all the exciting changes: the haircut, the shampoo, flushing the toilet, using the telephone, visiting friends, and sleeping each night in his bed. "The usual" had drifted down to only three juices instead of four, plus milk, and Sammy fixed it himself. He showered and changed his clothes once a week, on Saturdays. He was also able to go to the weekly math team practice.

"And I found a loophole," added Sammy, the lawyer's son.

"A loophole?" Dr. Geller was puzzled.

"I don't *need* to do compulsions anymore," Sammy explained. "I just can't stop yet. They're too much of a habit. So instead I do a substitute compulsion."

"What would that be?" Dr. Geller leaned back in his chair.

"Like I count to six on my fingers instead of going over an

invisible wall." Sammy held his hands up and silently counted off. "See?" he asked.

"Good." Dr. Geller nodded. "Very good."

ONE WEEK AFTER OUR appointment with Dr. Geller, Josh was home for December break. *The Lord of the Rings* was playing in the theaters, and he wanted to see it. Sammy piped up to say that he wanted to go, too.

"Don't you think the battle scenes might be too much for you?" I didn't want to risk anything that might upset him.

"Mom, I read the book. It'll be okay."

Sammy rarely left the house, and he had not wanted to see a movie for a year and a half. I seized the moment and hustled them into the van. In the parking lot after the movie, I opened the driver's door of the van and flicked the button that unlocked all the doors.

"Hey, Mom!" Sammy called over from the passenger side of the van. I knew he wanted me to come slide the door open for him.

"Can you get it for him, Josh?" I called over.

There was a moment of quiet conversation between the boys before I heard back from Josh.

"I think you need to come, Mom," Josh called back.

"Be right there . . . ," I called back. I'd given up trying to understand Sammy's quirks. Apparently he needed me—not Josh—to open the door, so I walked around to the other side of the van. The three boys were waiting, Sammy by the sliding door.

"Watch!" he shouted; then he gleefully grabbed the handle of the van door and slid it open.

I screamed with delight. I had to hold myself back from smothering him with kisses, which was the opposite of all my motherly instincts and it drove me crazy—but this time, the joy made up for it. I grabbed James in a bear hug and swung him around.

The next day, Sammy came outside to help me shovel snow.

"Let's go inside," Sammy called after about twenty minutes.

"Just let me finish this part," I called back. I was scraping away some snow that had fallen from a tree on the far side of the van.

"Mom, let's go in, now!"

I was concerned by the urgency in his voice and quickly hurried around to see what was up. Then I burst into tears.

Sammy, with a giant smile, stood on the porch holding open the front door. It was the first time he had touched it since we'd moved in, eighteen months before.

17

New Year

January and February are the coldest months in Maine. The days are short, and the winds are wicked. The ocean is frigid, and chunks of ice float on the marsh. The islands are colorless. The landscape is stark. The wildlife is mostly silent.

February will always be a warm month for me, though. It was the month when I knew in my heart that Sammy would be well.

THE NEW YEAR DAWNED full of promise.

Sammy still started his days with "the usual" and occasionally jabbered, but he continued to make consistent gains. He was able to explain many of his compulsions. We met periodically with the school to assess his progress. The school psychologist suggested that Sammy record his experiences. Sammy was excited and worked hard to get a dictation program up and running on his computer. He also talked about having his bar mitzvah.

"Before I turn fourteen," he clarified

"But, Sammy, that's only four months away."

"I know, Mom. I can do it!" he insisted.

"We'll see," I said.

He worked hard on overcoming his behaviors.

"Mom . . . come watch!" he called happily to me in my office.

I bounded down the stairs and then cheered as he paced back and forth across a mat, walked flat-footed through an invisible wall, or touched a different door handle. He did the task once and then increased the number of times on each subsequent day. He consistently opened the front door to the house and slid open the door to the van. He went outside of his own volition. With each gain, he became more confident.

"My bar mitzvah, Mom. I want to have it."

"Maybe," I answered.

I did not want to plan an event that might need to be postponed at the last minute if he fell apart. Guests would be coming from out of town. There would be air flights and hotel reservations to cancel. Then I remembered the birthday party for Leah's mother. It was set for the beginning of February, and family would be traveling to New York. Perhaps a ceremony could be coordinated with the party. If Sammy ended up being too ill to go through with it, canceling would not be a disaster. Leah was immediately supportive.

We decided on a short ceremony at the restaurant, just before the party. I gave it a fifty-fifty chance that Sammy would be well enough, but having the tentative plan and a solid goal spurred him on to greater gains. He doubled his efforts at mastering his behaviors.

We had moved his computer notebook to a station on the second floor. It made everything easier. When the tutor came, they spread his books across the kitchen table, and he could snack while they worked. I was just steps away if they needed anything. He began using the keyboard on a regular basis, and he frequently researched questions on the Internet. He also began working on his bar mitzvah speech. I knew from the questions he called out periodically that he was going to mention his illness.

"Mom," he called out, "how long was I sick before I saw Nicolaides?"

"About a year," I called back.

"And Geller, when did we see him? What month was that?"

"October," I answered. "Halloween day."

"That's right!" I heard, just before the persistent clicking of the keyboard resumed.

I started making invitations. Each day, while Sammy shed another compulsive behavior, I swirled fancy silver letters across deep blue cardboard. I wrote in all the information except the date and place, just in case we had to save them to use another time. For each invitation, I made a small, separate white card that read, "Sammy prefers a handshake instead of a hug."

Dr. Nicolaides was pleased with everything she saw during our January visit. By then, Sammy was taking 2,000 milligrams of Augmentin XR, 10 milligrams of Zyprexa, and 40 milligrams of Strattera. We talked about trying to lower the Augmentin but decided to wait until after the bar mitzvah.

"He's so much better. Do you still think we should see the neurologist at the Floating Hospital?" I asked.

"Can't hurt," she answered.

IN THE 1890S, the Floating Hospital was a boat that offered care for sick children while it cruised through Boston Harbor. The theory was that the salt air might promote speedier recovery. Although it evolved into a traditional hospital building, it kept the name. Sammy and I were there at the end of January. A nurse led us into a small examination room where the neurologist waited. He was thumbing through the many pages of historical information I had sent in advance.

"Oh good, you got my package," I said as we walked in.

The doctor looked up. "My worst fear was that you would bring more notes."

This doctor spent a great deal of time reviewing the history and examining Sammy. He was kind and patient. He tested Sammy's reflexes, tossed a ball with him in the hall, and reviewed the volumes of paperwork. At the conclusion, Sammy waited in the hall while the doctor spoke privately with me.

"There's no neurological damage," he stated. "He's awkward, but he just needs practice."

I nodded.

"But I don't think its PANDAS," he continued. "I've seen lots and lots of cases of PANDAS, and this isn't it. He has OCD. The best thing you can do for him is to accept that diagnosis."

"Even though he never got better until we treated it as PANDAS?" I asked.

"Coincidence. OCD symptoms come and go."

I smiled politely and thanked him. On the ride back to Maine, I brought Sammy up to date.

"If it's not PANDAS, how come I never got better when we treated it for a year as OCD?" Sammy asked as we crossed the bridge over the Piscataqua River and landed in Maine.

"Because it *is* PANDAS; he's mistaken," I said, recalling the phrase about truth coming from the mouths of babes.

"Nice doctor, though," Sammy added.

"Very nice man," I agreed.

"Can you turn the radio up?"

"Sure." I reached for the knob.

ONE WEEK LATER, we were at Dr. Geller's for our February visit.

"I still think it's PANDAS," he said after politely listening to my report about our visit to the neurologist.

It was two days before the bar mitzvah, and the invitations had been mailed. Dr. Geller was interested in all the arrangements, and Sammy gave him a copy of his bar mitzvah speech.

"Good." He nodded, then pointed us in the direction we needed to go next: more time with friends, more school interaction, more time outside, more exercise. Dr. Geller is a "big picture" guy. He always pushed us gently forward, while taking a quick look back to recognize the scope of the gains.

There are some people who can do more for you in an hour than others can do in a lifetime. Dan Geller and Cathy Nicolaides play in that ballpark.

SAMMY'S BAR MITZVAH was scheduled for a Saturday night.

"Dad's coming, isn't he?" Sammy asked after school on

Friday, as we started off on our drive south, which would go like a breeze.

"Of course, love. He's probably there already," I answered.

The children's paternal uncle and aunt, ever supportive, had invited us all to stay with them in New York City. It was challenging for me to spend time with my ex-husband, but I managed because it was important to and for Sammy.

After the kids were asleep, the adults discussed the plans for the next day's events. Sammy's dad wanted to keep the details of Sammy's illness private. He was concerned that Sammy might be embarrassed if we shared much information about what he had been through.

"Why don't we take our lead from Sammy?" I suggested, and he agreed.

About fifty people gathered together that evening at the waterfront restaurant. The Manhattan skyline twinkled in the background as the rabbi led the prayers. Sammy had worked hard on his Hebrew for the abbreviated ceremony, and he did a very good job. Then it was time for his speech. As I watched Sammy unfold his paper and prepare to begin, I'd never felt prouder or more confident. Leah, sitting beside me, took my hand. It was a lively group. But midway through the second sentence, you could have heard a pin drop.

I've had some problems for a while now. Stepping over invisible walls, holding my breath, and keeping things even were the first things.

When we moved from our old rental house in Maine to a new house that we owned, I had mixed feelings. On one level, I liked the nice house, and I could see that Mom was glad that she finally owned something in Maine. On another level, I really missed the old house. But the main problem with moving was that it seemed to intensify my behaviors after a little while.

I've stepped over invisible walls for a very long time. I don't remember quite how long, I can see them somehow. I wish I could tell you when I started holding my breath, but I can't remember that, too. In the new house, there were more invisible walls, I had to hold my breath when going from the first to the second floor, and I could not go through the front door of the house. In the old house, the worst it ever got was me hating to look at bare feet. After we moved, sometimes I couldn't even leave my room. Couldn't eat. Couldn't do much of anything. I was constantly having emotional breakdowns, and it was apparent that there was definitely something wrong. So I was heading to a doctor, a psychologist, hopefully he could help me.

It's funny, you know, although I had all these problems I could never talk about them. I would stay in my room, locked up, never leaving. Boiling in the middle of summer with the windows closed, I would never tell anyone why I was doing this. The windows, well, that breeze I just couldn't stand it. Somehow that breeze really disagreed with me. It was another thing that made it so I couldn't eat. It was becoming unbearable. I had to tell someone, but I couldn't, because the first and foremost rule was that I couldn't tell a soul. I couldn't eat when the windows were open, I couldn't eat when I saw bare feet, I couldn't even eat if the sounds of my eating corresponded with some other sounds. So I stayed in my room almost forever. That almost forever was really only a couple of months, but it seemed like forever to me.

It was in July that we went to see the psychologist. It took me forever to get downstairs. I went to countless meetings with him, but it didn't help enough, I just didn't seem to get better. Then the psychologist suggested a new doctor, a psychiatrist, Dr. Drill.

Drill suggested that I had obsessive-compulsive disorder and it was related to a lack of serotonin. He recommended Zoloft. He said this would help. This serotonin reuptake inhibitor, Zoloft, helped a bit but no matter how much we increased it, it could not solve the problem. I didn't know what to do. I was lost. It must've taken at least three months before Drill decided it was a dopamine situation as well. I hated the idea of adding a new medicine; I just couldn't stand it. Something was wrong. I could tell. When a person who worked for my grandmother said it could be related to strep, I somehow knew that was it. But Drill didn't know enough about it. Nonetheless, we decided to get a strep titer blood test. It turns out I had elevated strep levels; which meant it truly was related to strep.

I'd been sick for a year when we set off to see a doctor in New Jersey. When we got to the hotel, it took me over two hours just to get into the hotel room. This was all related to touching a small squirt gun, which I despised, a week or so before. When my foot made contact with it, it instantly triggered a behavior where I always had to have both feet touching something, generally both feet on or off the ground. This wasn't always that hard, but the hardest part was going over invisible walls, as you well can guess, I had to hop over them. The next day was equally hard. When we finally got into the doctor in New Jersey's office she gave me a full physical but didn't run any other tests. I didn't know it yet, but she was going to make things a lot better.

In September, the doctor in New Jersey told us to see a new doctor, a Boston doctor. He happened to be a world-renowned doctor. On October 31st we were off to see him. When we first stepped into his waiting room, we were surprised at the size. It was a tad smaller than other waiting rooms. It had three chairs, and a very nice chandelier. The wait seemed like an eternity. When we finally got in, it looked like it would be worth it. I can't quite recall what he said in that conversation, but I know it was very comforting. He seemed to agree with the doctor in New Jersey and told us not to change anything. I left feeling quite good.

Now, with hard work and help from the doctor in New Jersey, the psychologist, and the Boston doctor, I'm finally getting better. I don't know how much longer this will last. Things may have gotten worse in the middle. But I'm finally getting better. I feel like now I can take control of my life.

Sammy finished and looked up from his paper, beaming. Every teary eye was riveted on him. The group sat in stunned silence, then erupted into a firestorm of cheering and clapping. When the prayers and blessings concluded, the family swarmed him, wanting to sweep him into its collective arms. Then, remembering the "handshake instead of a hug" note, they extended their hands to him and hugged one another instead. Sammy relentlessly counted to six on his fingers as a substitute for whatever compulsion the physical contact of so many handshakes triggered. His grandmother had a tough time not pulling him into a hug. His dad stood proudly in the middle of a throng of well-wishers.

"Who wrote his speech?" one of his cousins came up to me and asked.

"He did."

"The whole thing?" She sounded doubtful.

"Every word." I nodded.

Leah's cousin embraced me. "In my entire life, I have never been to a more moving bar mitzvah. I've never seen anything like it."

"Beth, it was . . . it was . . ." My ex-sister-in-law hugged me while she struggled to find the right word. "Extraordinary."

The words I heard again and again were "amazing," "unbelievable," and "never before."

After the dinner celebration for Leah's mother, the toasts began. James patiently waited in line and then took his turn at the microphone. He spoke up clearly in that sweet, high-pitched, nine-year-old voice of his.

"I just want to say about Sammy—sometimes it was *reeeaaally* hard for me." Then he stopped, not sure what to say next.

The guests burst out laughing and then into applause.

At brunch the next morning, Sammy's remarkable speech was the number one topic of conversation. Relatives asked for copies by mail. Leah's husband had me describe in more detail the obstacles Sammy had overcome.

With a full stomach and a warm heart, I stood outside and watched a group of cousins sled down a backyard hill. Sammy was with them, another accomplishment. I remembered the hours he had spent in front of his computer, working and reworking that speech until he was satisfied with every word.

One of the California cousins broke into my thoughts. "Beth, your boys are really good sledders!"

"Well, I hope so. We live in Maine!" I giggled.

By noon, I was anxious to get on the road. It was a long drive north, and by four-thirty it would be dark. I dislike driving in the dark at the end of a long day. It's one thing when there is someone to help, but I was on my own. My ex-sister-in-law helped me get the kids and our packages together. We made the rounds of hugs and kisses and worked our way out the door. A collection of relatives stood nearby to wish us well. My boys and I climbed into the van and buckled our seat belts.

"Dad, c'mon, we're leaving!" James shouted, waving from his seat. "Come say good-bye again!"

His dad ran over and poked his head through the opening left by the sliding door on Sammy's side.

"Bye, boys . . ." He patted Sammy on the leg and smiled. "Nice speech!"

"Thank you!" Sammy smiled back.

Then the boys' dad stepped back onto the sidewalk, Sammy slid the door shut, and we were off.

18

A Fragile Balance

Augmentin is an extremely powerful antibiotic that is often prescribed when penicillin is not effective. It is largely composed of penicillin, but it also contains something called clavulanic acid. Clavulanic acid prevents the breakdown of penicillin; it makes the penicillin more effective. I often wondered why Augmentin had worked for Sammy when so many other powerful antibiotics had failed him.

I started thinking about inflammation in Sammy's brain after I read an article in the *New York Times* about Alzheimer's and Augmentin. It reported that when a group of Alzheimer's patients were given daily doses of Augmentin, their memories improved. The article quoted experts who theorized the possibility of inflammation in the patients' brains. I also had anecdotal information about elderly patients who made remarkable recoveries when fluid was released from their brains. Perhaps fluid on the brain creates a pressure similar to swelling. The body swelled when it was pounded; why not the brain when assaulted by antibodies? Could this be the "mental itch" that had caused Sammy to bang his head when he first got sick?

Dr. Nicolaides believes there is something to the anti-inflammatory premise. One of her PANDAS patients, who also suffered from asthma, had his OCD symptoms abate when he took prednisone for the asthma. Prednisone is a steroid that is also an anti-inflammatory. As the prednisone was withdrawn, the OCD symptoms returned. This led her to believe that there was inflammation in the basal ganglia. She wondered if perhaps swelling is caused when the antibodies and antigens react.

My experience with Dr. Nicolaides is that she is always right.

I TOOK THE KIDS to Florida for the February school break. Sammy was in the ocean every day. He decided to work on his aversion to bare feet. He started wearing pajamas again. I took long walks on the beach. I finally felt comfortable leaving the three of them alone. I no longer anticipated a crisis. Sometimes when I walked, I spontaneously burst into tears and cried for twenty minutes. I was shedding all the sadness that had bound me for so long.

Sammy and I were in the ocean together early one afternoon toward the end of the week. The air was warm, and the sun was gentle. There was a bit of a bump to the sea. We bounced around, jumping and diving waves together. It was on earlier trips to the deliciously warm waters of Florida that I had taught my boys how to dive waves—the same way my father had taught me at the Jersey Shore when I was little.

There were lots of dips and crevices on the ocean floor. We laughed, because we kept losing our balance. Suddenly I burst into tears, aware that we were sharing a moment I'd feared might never come. Sammy popped up from a wave and looked over.

"You're crying again, aren't you?" He bobbed up and down with the surf.

I nodded yes.

"You don't need to cry anymore, Mom. It's over."

I believed him and cried even harder.

Sammy had no compulsions in Florida: no hopping, no stepping over invisible walls, no tics. As soon as we returned, they all came rushing back.

He crawled through the spot between the door and the couch, stepped over invisible walls, ducked when he passed the television, and hopped in other places. He cleared his throat, swirled his head, and blinked his eyes. The verbal tics were so ferocious that I could hear them behind closed doors.

"It's back," he said with eyes full of fear.

"It'll be okay," I said reassuringly and tried not to let panic overwhelm me.

The behaviors multiplied. Was the home we had grown to love poisoned from the memories of his illness? Suddenly, inspiration struck. Perhaps he needed some help breaking those miserable habits. I moved all the furniture while he slept. I pushed the couches into different configurations and blocked where he used to crawl. I moved all the floor mats to different places. He had mentioned a ray for an invisible wall coming out of a small red light at the bottom of a television. I stuck that TV in the closet. When he woke up, everything was different, and my idea worked. He stopped crawling and hopping and stepping over walls.

The behaviors stopped, but the verbal tics continued. I hoped they would spontaneously subside, but they grew worse. Every sentence was broken by a tic. We went to another meeting at school. He read his bar mitzvah speech for the team of administrators and teachers who were following his academic and social progress. When he finished, the room was wrapped in the same, stunned silence as at the ceremony. Then the team members burst into applause. Their frame of reference was his improvement from our last meeting, but mine was the nearly flawless reading he'd given at the bar mitzvah. This time his talk was peppered with tics. I saw his head jerk back and thought how scary it must be for him to have the tics altering his speech pattern again.

If he's worried about the tics, I thought as I watched, *that will make them worse.* Anxiety increases compulsions.

On the way home, I said casually, "Hey, I did some research on tics last night. It says more tics come in the cold weather. We were just in Florida, so that's a big change in temperature. Once you're used to the cold, they'll subside, so don't worry about it."

By one in the afternoon, the throat tics were gone. The rest of the tics were a memory within a week.

IN MARCH, SOUTHWEST STARTED flying from Manchester, New Hampshire, to Philadelphia for twenty-nine dollars each way. Manchester is ninety minutes from Kennebunkport, and Dr. Nicolaides's office is less than one hour from the Philadelphia airport. It cost me less to fly and rent a car than it did to drive, not to mention the savings on personal wear and tear. Plus, I always find it fun to hop on a plane.

"Did I enable him by moving the furniture?' I asked Dr. Nicolaides.

"It's one of the best ideas I've ever heard," she answered.

Then we went through my journal, watched my tapes, and decided to cut the Augmentin XR in half. If all went well, after three or four weeks, we would halve it again. The Zyprexa and Strattera dosages would remain unchanged.

When we got back from Philly, I decided it was time to get started on my promise to God. A day later, an e-mail came from the Maine State Bar Association about the annual summer meeting. It was going to be in Bar Harbor in June, and the organizers were canvassing members for program ideas.

My goal became getting Dr. Nicolaides in front of the group. My thinking was that guardians *ad litem* need to understand children's mental health issues in order to be more effective. I'd had little understanding of the whole mental health piece before my experience with Sammy. Perhaps we could empower attorneys to ask the right questions. The president of the bar association liked my idea, so I began to fill my nonexistent empty hours with the task of putting a presentation together.

Simultaneously, I tracked Sammy on the reduced Augmentin. It took about ten days before there were any changes; then he started having short emotional breakdowns. This was the first time I had seen breakdowns since we'd tried to lower the dose four months earlier. I faxed Dr. Nicolaides every other day to bring her up to speed. Sammy knew about the reduction.

This time, he was well enough to help guide us, so my faxes included his input.

"What shall I tell her?" I asked him.

"Tell her, word for word, I can feel the symptoms there— barely there—but the way I feel is just different." He paused. "If it stays like this, it's fine. I can shake it off at any time. But it's different. I can't really describe it . . . just a feeling in my gut."

We ran a blood test. His strep titer came in at 400, so I watched him like a hawk. The next weeks were tough, but he was determined to stay at the half dose of 1,000 milligrams of Augmentin XR and see if he could manage the symptoms. There was never a crisis, but he cycled with tears, a slightly stiffer walk, sudden outbursts of anger, and struggling around the tutoring and schoolwork. One morning he'd say that all was well. A few days later he might say the strep was coming back, or be angry and slam doors. The only consistency was the absence of compulsions; it was all emotional.

Thirty days after the reduction, the emotional breakdowns were gone. I mentioned to Sammy the possibility of cutting the Augmentin further.

"Not right now," he said. "It's a fragile balance, and I don't want to do anything to mess it up."

We put the plan for further reductions on hold, and April rolled along happily. The gains came by leaps and bounds.

"Mom, come see!" he'd call to me in my office.

I'd gleefully spring down the steps to see the latest accomplishments. He'd proudly walk upstairs without holding his breath. Or he'd flick a light switch, or open and close the door he'd asked me to take off its hinges months earlier.

"Sammy!" I'd give him the thumbs-up sign, wanting desperately to tackle him in a hug.

His weekly trips to math team practice were no longer painful. At school, he hopped a few lines in the crosswalk and jumped over some patterns in the floor, but it was nothing more than ordinary quirkiness. At the end of April, his math team coach sent me an e-mail: "Beth, I am absolutely delighted with Sammy's performance. He has qualified for the BIG math meet in May."

"Sammy, look at this!" I handed him the e-mail. "You deserve a treat. I'm going to Colonial. Can I get you something at the Candy Man?"

"The Candy Man is open?" he asked.

"Yes, it is."

"I think I'll come and pick it out myself," he answered.

When we parked at Dock Square, Sammy stepped out of the van and stood still for a minute. He looked around slowly at the charming clapboard buildings that frame the square.

"Wow!" he said. "I haven't been here for a *long* time."

While I went for his medicine, Sammy walked around the corner to the Candy Man all by himself.

TOWARD THE END OF April, Josh came home for spring break. His second year at boarding school had been a great success. I excitedly filled him in about all the developments and wrapped up with the plan to possibly reduce the Augmentin further.

"Do you think you could wait until I go back to school?" he asked hesitantly.

I laughed and agreed.

Sammy had an occasional bad day throughout April, but it was hard to tell if it was due to the disorder or adolescence. One day, he said he could remember when he was really sick and his eyesight blacked over for a full second. I'd had no idea that anything like that had ever happened. Another day, he cried during tutoring and said he felt like the tremor was back. A different day, he said, "Everything I do is a struggle." But most days went smoothly, and every so often he would say that it was over.

Jim was in California for meetings about a miniseries he wanted to write and direct. He kept in touch regularly to find out how Sammy was doing.

"Let me know how he does at the meet. And you should write a book," he e-mailed me one day. "I mean it."

I remembered what he'd said about true stories, years earlier, when we'd stood on that sunny tennis court by the Pacific.

MAY BLOOMED BRILLIANTLY WITH hope for the future. Sammy's schoolwork moved along at a nice clip. Sunny days brought kayaking. And Sammy looked forward to competing in the biggest math meet of the year.

He started the morning of the math meet without "the usual." He had eliminated it earlier in the week. He woke up in his bed, in his pajamas, and then took a shower. He walked out the front door, let himself into the van, and hummed a tune on our drive to the Portland Expo.

"Look, there they are!" We had reached the Expo, and he pointed to the bus carrying his teammates.

It was in the middle of a lineup of school buses whose engines were idling at the curb. Twenty-five schools, both public and private, were members of the Southern Maine Math League. Four times a year, the big yellow buses rolled up for the meets. Hundreds of kids, math skills as sharp as their pencils, filed off and into the Expo. The May math meet included grades five through eight. Each school, at each grade level, sent a team of six members. Some teams wore matching T-shirts covered with equations and symbols or with slogans like "Mathlete = Problem Child" or "Have Your Pi and Eat It, Too."

We pulled past the Expo and parked. Sammy hurried out of our van and after his teammates. Once inside, he walked through the lobby and over the mud mats without hopping or jumping or swirling his legs. He did not hold his breath. He weaved his way among the hundreds of folding tables, searching for the seventh-grade section and the table tagged "Middle School of the Kennebunks."

"Sammy, over here!" Devers called across the din.

The entire team broke out in smiles as Sammy headed for the table. A couple of its members stood and waved. He took a seat on one of the folding chairs.

Each table was divided into separate workstations by large, tall pieces of corrugated cardboard that would be removed for the team round. He joked with his teammates while they waited for the chair of the Southern Maine Math League to call the meet to order. The noise level was deafening, as the voices of six hundred student competitors ricocheted off the cavernous ceiling.

With everyone in his or her place, the chair stepped to the podium and spoke into the microphone she held in her hand.

"QUIET, PLEASE, QUIET."

Sammy started to quiet down with the rest of them, but there was still quite a bit of noise.

"MAY I HAVE YOUR ATTENTION PLEASE!" Her voice boomed through the public address system in a very no-nonsense tone.

The students settled down. The chair reviewed the rules. Teacher and parent proctors distributed test papers.

"IS THERE ANYONE WITHOUT A PAPER?"

A few hands shot up. Proctors scurried to their sides, and then we all waited for the moment when everyone was ready.

"YOU MAY BEGIN!"

Silence descended, except for the sound of six hundred flipping papers. Proctors, including me, walked silently among the tables. There was no talking, not even a whisper. Only the quiet scratch of pencils working out computations on the scrap paper that rested on each table. The large electronic clock counted down the fifteen minutes of each round.

"TWO MINUTES," the chair announced precisely when the clock read 2:00 in big, red, square numbers.

"PENCILS DOWN!" she announced when the squares reached 0:00.

The students' voices exploded through the Expo at the conclusion of each round.

After the individual rounds, the cardboard dividers were disassembled and moved to the back of the Expo. This enabled the team members to work together on the problems for the team round.

When the team round was over and all the papers were collected, the students rushed for the sides of the Expo. Parent volunteers, including Devers's mom, Chris, staffed long tables stocked with cookies and juice. The competitors munched and talked computations, while teachers on the second floor scored the papers. After twenty minutes, the chair moved back to the microphone.

"MAY I HAVE YOUR ATTENTION PLEASE!"

Sammy grabbed an extra sugar cookie and hurried back to the tables, along with all the other students. Then the six hundred students all fell quiet, waiting to hear the winners announced. Excitement and anticipation bounced off the walls like static electricity.

I fiddled with my video camera. I wanted to show Dr. Nicolaides what a math meet actually looked like. I had already filmed the outside of the Expo, the mud mats that Sammy used to jump, the room full of competitors and tables, and the electronic score clock. I hoped Sammy would win an award so I could show her that, too.

The awards started with third place for fifth grade and moved up from there. Fern, the grade school's teacher for the gifted program, was there with her fifth-grade team. I was happy when one of her students placed. Individual awards were always announced first, followed by the winning teams. Sammy listened to his iPod while the fifth and sixth graders were called up for their awards. When the last sixth-grade team wrapped up, I motioned for him to take the buds out of his ears. I wanted him to be ready in case he won. He'd made astonishing gains in the last week, so I hoped that maybe, just maybe, he'd have another feather to add to his cap.

"AND FOR THE SEVENTH GRADE . . . ," the chair began.

I practiced my zoom and worked on holding the camera steady.

Sammy did not get third place. I calmed myself with thoughts of second place but watched it go elsewhere, too. I stood there, video camera at my side, trying hard to be a good sport about the whole thing. After all, he was there in one piece, without compulsions, competing with his teammates. I was grateful for that; perhaps hoping for more was greedy. Then the chair began again.

"AND IN FIRST PLACE, FOR THE SEVENTH GRADE . . ."

The kids were getting noisy, so she paused. I held my breath and waited.

"FROM THE MIDDLE SCHOOL OF THE KENNEBUNKS . . ."

When I heard the name of Sammy's school, I knew it had to be him, and I burst into tears.

"WITH A PERFECT PAPER . . . SAAAAAAM-EEEEE . . ."

I was crying so hard by "perfect paper" that I did not hear the chair finish Sammy's name. He leapt from his seat and walked proudly to the front of the room. I hooted and hollered over all the commotion. It was all I could do to keep from jumping up and down. His teammates stood up and cheered. The math team coach waved over to me and smiled. Chris, grinning ear to ear, shot me two thumbs up from the snack tables. Fern, nodding, clapped hard with her hands above her head. I did my best to pull the video camera up and record it all, but I had a tough time seeing through my tears.

When Sammy moved over to have his picture taken for the

newspaper, I pressed Jim's number on my cell phone. My finger shook with emotion. When he picked up, I shouted over the roar, hoping he could hear me.

"He won the meet, Jim! He had a perfect paper. Can you hear me? He's back! I've really got him back!"

19

Life Begins Again

In Cape Porpoise, Maine, at the side of the harbor, on the last tip of land, is the pier. In the summertime, the beauty and glory are palpable. Gulls swoop and glide. Lobstermen unload their catches. Dinghies crowd the dock.

At the mouth of the harbor, a buoy clangs. Its song drifts in on the breeze. Dogs bark, gulls caw, children call to their mothers. Halyards clink against sailboat masts. Stripers race in on the tide.

On warm, friendly evenings, pink-fingered clouds stretch across the sky and touch the harbor with their graceful points. Sometimes a rainbow dips into the sea where—beyond the harbor, beyond the lighthouse—the North Atlantic beckons to my heart and soul.

I lead a charmed and blessed life.

THE SUMMER OF SAMMY'S recovery stretches out in my memory like one long kayaking adventure across a golden sea.

The entries in my journal start to dwindle during May, then fade to nonexistent.

Justine and I rode up to the bar association meeting together in early June. She was pregnant again. I was not worried about leaving the boys with a sitter this time. I knew that all would be well.

Dr. Nicolaides was a featured speaker for the full-day program "Children's Mental Health Issues." Justine and I had dinner with her the night before the presentation. It felt good to be working on my promise. When I looked out from the panel the next day, I spotted the chief justice of the Maine Supreme Court in the audience.

THE KIDS AND I took a short camping trip to Martha's Vineyard that summer. Sharon's daughter was having her bat mitzvah there. Sammy had no difficulty sleeping in the cabin.

When we got home, he and his brothers returned with Devers to their beloved rocket camp. I drove the morning shift, and Chris drove the afternoon. Each day, Sammy was quicker about getting into the van. He did not miss a single day of camp.

After rocket camp ended, the tutor came back. Our goal was to have Sammy complete the seventh-grade curriculum by the end of the summer. He could then rejoin his former class in eighth grade. It would be a push, but he was determined to meet the goal. I was uneasy about sending him back to school, worried that it might set him back.

The director of special education eased my concerns. "You've got to let him try," she encouraged. "If it doesn't work, we'll figure it out then." Our school system was always there for us.

Sammy continued with the weekly counseling sessions and worked hard on his few remaining behaviors. At home, when he wasn't concentrating on his schoolwork or on programming the computer game he had created at rocket camp, he wandered the neighborhood shoeless. Bare feet—on him or anyone else—were no longer a problem. He wore clothing of any color. He showered regularly and slept in his bed every night.

Sammy started joking about what he had been through. If I asked him how he felt, he'd jerk around wildly, shake his head, and roll his eyes before shouting out, "Fine! Why?" For breakfast, he wanted "Putttt, putttt, pancakes." He demonstrated fake mood swings in response to dinner suggestions. "Chicken!" he'd shout excitedly, then pretend to sob before breaking into a laugh.

He was taking 10 milligrams of Zyprexa and 40 milligrams of Strattera. We tried, once again, to lower the Augmentin to 500 milligrams per day. Sammy did better this time. Almost two months passed before the compulsions came back. First, he said that things were getting "hard." Next, he said he was having a compulsion that involved a stomach muscle. Then he stopped flushing the toilet and started counting on his fingers again. I wanted to play it out for as long as possible. I thought the backsliding might be attributable to anxiety due to a busy summer. But when he took three steps over an invisible wall, I called Dr. Nicolaides immediately. I was scared to death.

"It's the Augmentin," she said, unperturbed. "Put it back up."

We went back to 1,000 milligrams of Augmentin XR. Within twenty-four hours, the bloom was back in his cheeks. Within forty-eight hours, the compulsions were completely gone.

IT WAS TOUGH for me to keep much straight that summer except for Sammy's meds and the tide chart. Otherwise, my brain was on extended vacation. I turned up in the wrong courthouses, on the wrong dates, at the wrong times. After being on overload for so long, I was experiencing forced shutdown.

My personal goal for the summer was to spend as much time as possible kayaking, bicycling, and seeing my friends. I had learned that life could change at any moment, and I was determined to live it to its best.

Jim was directing his miniseries that summer. He e-mailed from location to check on Sammy's progress. "Did you start a book yet?" he typed one day. "You have to, about all this. We'll make a movie."

Josh was behind the movie idea if Angelina Jolie would star. While we traveled to tour college campuses, he suggested story revisions that included wet T-shirts. Carnegie Mellon was his favorite, and he decided to apply for early decision.

James spent the summer in constant motion. After rocket camp, he ran around at arts camp for a week. Then he ran off with the local Parks and Recreation program. He did everything: field trips, tennis lessons, mini golf, regular golf, archery, and soccer.

Dr. Geller sent me to meet with Sammy's team of teachers over the summer. He wanted to make certain that they understood what Sammy had been through, and that the *only* goal for eighth grade was for him to show up. Academic success or failure could not be part of the agenda. He said it might be hard for them to accept that, because all teachers want their students to succeed academically.

"I know; my mother was a teacher," Dr. Geller added thoughtfully.

When I met with them, I brought along copies of pages from my journal so that they could see where we had been and how far we had come. I took them through the long, painful two-year history and gave them a copy of the bar mitzvah speech.

"Tell Sammy," said the team leader, Mr. Bibeau, at the end of the meeting, "that after what he has been through, it will be an honor to teach him."

I blinked back tears.

Toward the end of the summer, Sammy progressed to putting the finishing touches on the computer game he'd been programming.

"How's it going?" I'd just come in from kayaking. I stood behind him and looked at the screen.

"Pretty well," Sammy answered.

"Who's that?" I pointed to a figure on the screen.

"That's the character who's in danger."

"And that one?" I pointed to another.

"That's the mom." Sammy stopped tapping the keyboard and turned in his chair to face me. "She's a great fighter who saves the character's life."

SAMMY FINISHED UP the seventh-grade curriculum with his tutor two weeks before the start of eighth grade. We made a trip back to New Jersey to see Dr. Nicolaides. We wanted her final okay for him to begin school. Sammy walked through the airport and then the halls of the Doubletree, just like any other traveler. We had dinner at the food court at the mall. He did not hop any lines or jump any patterns.

The next day, Dr. Nicolaides reviewed all of his progress and gave him her seal of approval.

"Can I rely on this? Will he ever be sick again?" I asked with a mixture of hope and dread.

"It's possible he'll get sick again," she answered honestly, "but he'll never go back to where he was."

Then suddenly we were home, and the beginning of school was just a few days away. Everyone at the middle school was prepped and ready for Sammy's arrival. A teacher was assigned to make sure that he made it off the bus and into the building. I called the school's transportation department to let them know that Sammy was coming back, that he might have a hard time, and that the driver needed to be patient and kind. The school had all my phone numbers: office, home, cell phone, and pager. The principal knew I would be there on a moment's notice. I canceled all court appearances, meetings, and kayaking for the day. At last, everything was in order.

I called my mom. "I think we're ready," I told her.

"Certainly sounds like it," she said.

THE FIRST DAY OF school dawned bright and sunny. Sammy and I had pancakes for breakfast and then walked to the bus stop together. We waited in the same spot where James and I had stood day after day for two years, hoping that Sammy would get well. The bus pulled up. Sammy got on. I waved as it pulled away. I stood and watched for a long time—feeling empty—as the yellow square disappeared down the road toward Cape Porpoise. Walking slowly home, I saw my neighbor Nancy in her yard. I detoured to say hello.

"Big day. Sammy went back to school!" I burst into tears and giggled at the same time.

She gave me a hug and said it would be okay.

I went home and woke James to get him ready. After breakfast, we walked out and waited for his bus.

It was a spectacular day. The sky was blue, and the clouds were bold. By ten, I had set up a beach chair in the side yard, with the telephones lined up next to me. The pager was hooked to my shorts. While I waited for the inevitable call, I had a lot of reading to do. I hoped he might at least make it to lunch. When it got to be one in the afternoon, I thought maybe he might make it through the day. At two, I moved everything into the house and sat down next to the telephone. I figured they would call at two-thirty to tell me that he could not get on the bus.

At three, I was still sitting on the couch, staring at the telephone. It was the same couch where Sammy had lain buried under cushions for months, where Peter had picked him up and carried him out the front door, where we had found his pills hidden in the cracks, and where he had lain motionless, too weak to move, while he'd listened to the tutor read. Then I looked out the door and saw Sammy strolling up the driveway. I could not see his face because he was looking down, kicking a stone.

I stood up, walked over to the front door, and pushed it

open. The same door he had been unable to use for almost two years.

"Sammy," I called out tentatively from the doorway, "how did school go?"

Sammy looked up from the stone he was kicking, a giant smile beaming on his face.

"Good," he said. "School was good, Mom."

Then he walked through the front door, and the nightmare was over.

After

Sammy remained on 1,000 milligrams of Augmentin XR for the next three years. He'd been tapered off the Zyprexa by the middle of ninth grade. The Strattera, at 40 milligrams, is still in place.

Two months after ceasing the Augmentin, he entered boarding high school as a junior at the Maine School of Science and Mathematics. Since its inception, the school has not seen a student with stronger math skills.

When I picked him up at the bus stop on his first trip home, he stood proud and tall. He was so happy to be well, living away from home, and managing his successful life.

"You look great! I wish I could hug you," I said as I hopped out of my Prius and opened the back for his suitcase.

"Go ahead, Mom—I'm over it." He shrugged and smiled back. "But the hugs won't be so special anymore if you get them all the time."

"Oh yes they will!" I said and reached out for the best hug of my life.

FOUR MONTHS AFTER Sammy entered boarding school, we had a scare. There had been a couple of strep outbreaks in his dorm. Each time he'd taken 1,000 milligrams of Augmentin XR for ten days, as a precaution. During the third outbreak, he called to say that something was wrong.

"It's the invisible walls," he told me. "They're back."

Two days prior, on a Wednesday, he'd caught himself swinging his leg over an outlet. He thought it might be the remnants of an old habit, but the next day, when he woke up, he could sense the walls everywhere. On Friday, he went to the school nurse.

"Are you scared, Sammy?" I tried to hold my voice steady while I calculated how quickly I could reach him. "Shall I come?"

"Nah. I'll just take more medicine, and they'll go away."

"Okay," I said brightly to disguise the terror in my heart.

We immediately upped the Augmentin XR to 2,000 milligrams a day.

I sobbed nonstop that weekend because I was so scared. I also took a lot of island walks and prayed. Walking on Sunday afternoon, I stopped to rest at one of my favorite spots. I stood on a boulder and gazed at the lighthouse, then looked down before stepping off. When I did, I sucked in a deep breath of that cold December air, because there at my feet rested a dark brown, porous rock unmistakably shaped like a heart. It was almost five inches long, four inches wide, and about an inch thick. A hairline crack divided the heart from top to bottom, and it was chipped on the right side, but it was solid. As I reached for it, I remembered something a friend had said earlier that year when we'd walked this same island: "All hearts are chipped."

I held that chipped heart gently in my hands, ran my finger along the crack, and then turned peacefully to take it home. I knew it was a sign that all would be well.

When I got back to the house, I called Sammy. He'd been on the medication for forty-eight hours.

"Are the walls still there?"

"Now that you mention it," he said, "I haven't noticed them today."

"So they're gone?"

"They're gone," he stated.

Dr. Nicolaides gradually reduced him to a maintenance dose of 500 milligrams a day and then weaned him off again.

A few weeks after the invisible walls had disappeared, Sammy was home for winter break. His report card arrived. He had earned straight A's for his first semester, and he could not wait to get back to school.

PANDAS WILL STICK WITH Sammy over the years. Maybe strep is buried deep in his system and resurfaces when he's reexposed. Maybe he picks up a new infection whenever one is around. Whichever it is, he'll manage it with antibiotics and continue to live a full life. He lost two years of that precious life, because doctors overlooked the possibility that an infection might be causing his mental illness. What if he had lost a lifetime?

Perhaps there's a child, suffering now, who will be helped because we shared what it took to save Sammy.

I'll be hoping for that, while I'm kayaking over the deep green sea and remembering my promise to God.

LAST, BUT NOT LEAST

SHORTLY AFTER Random House agreed to publish *Saving Sammy*, I had the opportunity to offer another mom the benefit of what I had learned through Sammy's experience.

Over lunch, she told me that her eleven-year-old had just been diagnosed with pervasive developmental disorder. PDD refers to a category of disorders; the diagnosis essentially means that the boy's issues affect virtually every area of his development. It is considered an autism spectrum disability.

"This has been going on for nine years," she said. "With the diagnosis, I'll finally be able to get him the services he needs."

I quietly wondered whether the doctors might have missed strep in this boy, too. As she ran through his symptoms—sensitivity to light, balance issues, speech delays—they bore no similarity to Sammy's behaviors. I was almost relieved. Then a thought struck me.

"Just out of curiosity, when's the last time he was on antibiotics?"

She silently ran through his medical history, then answered, "Not since he was sixteen months old. He had Lyme disease."

"Was his blood tested again, to make sure the Lyme was fully treated?" I asked.

"No," she answered. "They just gave him amoxicillin for a month, and that was it."

"In nine years, no doctor ever wondered if he might still be infected?" The wheels in my brain were spinning.

"No." She shook her head. "I brought it up a few times, but they dismissed it and said I didn't know how to parent.

A few years ago, he had a complete neurological evaluation, and that's what the neuropsychologist diagnosed: poor parenting."

"You need to have his blood tested—right away," I said. "Lyme invades the brain. Maybe he's still got it."

A few days later, I was golfing with a nurse. As I watched my ball sail into the woods, I asked her the current protocol for treating Lyme. She said that sometimes the antibiotics are delivered intravenously. I called my friend right after the game.

"You must have him tested," I urged.

About two weeks later, my friend e-mailed to say that she had researched late-stage Lyme. Her son's symptoms were consistent with everything she'd read. She had learned that there were only two labs in the country that specialize in blood tests for such patients. She had brought all the information to the pediatrician. He'd told her she was wrong and had refused to send the blood to the specialized lab.

"Don't you pay attention to him," I fired back, furious with the pediatrician. "You find another doctor."

With a lot of hard work, she located a physician with expertise in late-stage Lyme. The boy's blood was sent to the special lab in California. When my friend called to tell me the results, two months after we had shared lunch, chills shot up my spine.

"He's got an active Lyme infection," she said, choking back tears. "That's what's been wrong with him all along. And we found out because of you."

"We found out because of Sammy," I said. "Without him, I would not have known to ask the questions."

MY FRIEND'S EXPERIENCE has made me much less forgiving of the doctors who overlooked Sammy's infection. I had excused their oversight because of the "newness" of PANDAS, but Lyme is a well-known disease and still doctors failed—more accurately, refused—to make the connection. And that's why, before any child is placed on psychiatric medication, we must ask the questions: Could this be an infection? Could it be a virus or bacteria? Have we tested to be certain that there's no invasive cause?

We must not rely on anyone else to ask these questions for us, and we must keep asking them until we are satisfied with the answers. If we are told that the questions are not appropriate, if we feel embarrassed or uncomfortable for asking, or if we're summarily dismissed with "No, that's not it," then we must find another doctor. Because while I do not think that every mental illness is due to infection, the possibility of an invasive cause must truly be ruled out first.

Historically, mental illness was linked with infection. When Georges Gilles de la Tourette first identified his syndrome in the 1800s, it was closely linked to rheumatic fever, caused by strep antibodies attacking the heart. In the 1920s, tics swept the population following an outbreak of encephalitis.

Yet as mental illness moved under the dark cloak of psychoanalysis—and patients' mothers were often blamed—the door to finding an invasive cause was closed. The steadfast refusal of some doctors to reopen that door is disconcerting. Studies consistently report links. *Scientific American Mind* reported in 2008 that schizophrenia has been linked to the flu, bipolar disorder to herpes, autism to Lyme disease, and OCD to strep.

I understand that medicine is a science and that scientists like proof. But I also recall our pediatrician telling me about the many years it took for doctors to accept that stomach ulcers are caused by infections. I can't help but think about all those sick patients who suffered needlessly. And, of course, I think of my son. While I appreciate the patience of doctors who are exploring and researching, the bottom line is that my son and the children like him simply do not have time to wait.

Which is why I am grateful for Dr. Nicolaides and Dr. Geller, physicians who are willing to follow their heads and their hearts and who treated my son with the instincts of artists. Because it is doctors practicing the *art* of medicine who hold the power to change lives—along with the parents and children who never give up.

Find the right doctors, ask them the questions, and let me know how it turns out.

Beth
www.savingsammy.net

SELECTED REFERENCES

FOR THOSE READERS who want to delve more into PANDAS:

Achenbach, T. M., S. H. McConaughy, and C. T. Howell. "Child/Adolescent Behavioral and Emotional Problems: Implications of Cross-Informant Correlations for Situational Specificity." *Psychological Bulletin* 101 (1987): 213–32.

Allen, A. J., H. L. Leonard, and S. E. Swedo. "Case Study: A New Infection-Triggered, Autoimmune Subtype of Pediatric OCD and Tourette's Syndrome." *Journal of the American Academy of Child and Adolescent Psychiatry* 34 (1995): 307–11.

Belkin, L. "Can You Catch Obsessive Compulsive Disorder?" *New York Times Magazine,* May 22, 2005: 64–69.

Borowsky, I. W., S. Mozayeny, and M. Ireland. "Brief Psychosocial Screening at Health Supervision and Acute Care Visits." *Pediatrics* 112 (2003): 129–33.

Bradford-Hill, A. B. "The Environment and Disease: Association and Causation." *Proceedings of the Royal Society of Medicine* 58 (1965): 295–300.

Cardona, F., and G. Orefici. "Group A Streptococcal Infections and Tic Disorders in an Italian Pediatric Population." *Journal of Pediatrics* 138 (2001): 71–75.

Church, A. J., R. C. Dale, A. J. Lees, G. Giovannoni, and M. M. Robertson. "Tourette's Syndrome: A Cross Sectional Study to Examine the PANDAS Hypothesis." *Journal of Neurology, Neurosurgery, and Psychiatry* 74 (2003): 602–07.

DiBella, D., S. Erzegovesi, M. C. Cavallini, and L. Bellodi. "Obsessive-Compulsive Disorder, 5-TTLPR Polymorphism and Treatment Response." *Pharmacogenomics Journal* 2 (2002): 176–81.

Garvey, M. A., J. Giedd, and S. E. Swedo. "PANDAS: the Search for Environmental Triggers of Pediatric Neuropsychiatric Disorders; Lessons from Rheumatic Fever." *Journal of Child Neurology* 13 (1998): 413–23.

Garvey, M. A., S. J. Perlmutter, A. J. Allen et al. "A Pilot Study of Penicillin Prophylaxis for Neuropsychiatric Exacerbations Triggered by Streptococcal Infections." *Biological Psychiatry* 45 (1999): 1564–71.

Garvey, M. A., L. A. Snider, S. F. Leitman, R. Werden, and S. E. Swedo. "Treatment of Sydenham's Chorea with Intravenous Immunoglobulin, Plasma Exchange, or Prednisone." *Journal of Child Neurology* 20 (2005): 424–29.

Giedd, J. N., J. L. Rapoport, M. A. Garvey, S. Perlmutter, and S. E. Swedo. "MRI Assessment of Children with Obsessive-Compulsive Disorder or Tics Associated with Streptococcal Infection." *American Journal of Psychiatry* 157 (2000): 281–83.

Giedd, J. N., J. L. Rapoport, H. L. Leonard, D. Richter, and S. E. Swedo. "Case Study: Acute Basal Ganglia Enlargement and Obsessive-Compulsive Symptoms in an Adolescent Boy." *Journal of the American Academy of Child and Adolescent Psychiatry* 35 (1996): 913–15.

Goldberg, C. "Mental Ailments in Children Being Linked to Strep." *Boston Globe,* June 28, 2003: 1.

Heubi, C., and S. R. Shott. "PANDAS: Pediatric Autoimmune Neuropsychiatric Disorders Associated with Streptococcal Infections—An Uncommon, but Important Indication for Tonsillectomy." *International Journal of Pediatric Otorhinolaryngology* 67 (2003) 837–40.

"How Strep Triggers Obsessive Compulsive Disorder—New Clues"; http://www.nimh.nih.gov/science-news/2006/how-strep-triggers-obsessive-compulsive-disorder-new-clues.shtml.

Huerta, P. T., C. Kowal, L. A. DeGiogio, B. T. Volpe, and B. Diamond. "Immunology and Behavior: Antibodies After Emotion." *Proceedings of the National Academy of Sciences USA* 103 (2006): 678–83.

Inoff-Germain, G., R. S. Rodriguez, S. Torres-Alcantara, M. J. Diaz-Jimenez, S. E. Swedo, and J. L. Rapoport. "An Immunological Marker (D8/17) Associated with Rheumatic Fever as a Predictor of Childhood Psychiatric Disorders in a Community Sample." *Journal of Child Psychology and Psychiatry* 44 (2003): 782–90.

Kaplan, E. "PANDAS? Or PAND? Or Both? Or Neither? Assessing a (Possible?) Temporal or Pathogenic Relationship with the Group A Streptococcal Disease Complex." *Contemporary Pediatrics* 8 (2000): 81–96.

Kiessling, L. S., A. C. Marcotte, and L. Culpepper. "Antineuronal Antibodies in Movement Disorders." *Pediatrics* 92 (1993): 39–43.

Kirvan, C., S. E. Swedo, L. Snider, and M. Cunningham. "Antibody-Mediated Neuronal Cell Signaling Behavior and

Movement Disorders." *Journal of Neuroimmunology* 179 (2006): 173–79.

Klein, R. G. "Parent-Child Agreement in Clinical Assessment of Anxiety and Other Psychopathology: A Review." *Journal of Anxiety Disorders* 5 (1991): 187–98.

Kurlan, R., D. Johnson, E. Kaplan, and the Tourette Syndrome Study Group. "Streptococcal Infection and Exacerbations of Childhood Tics and Obsessive-Compulsive Symptoms: A Prospective Blinded Cohort Study." *Pediatrics* 121 (2008): 1188–97.

Kurlan, R., and E. L. Kaplan. "The Pediatric Autoimmune Neuropsychiatric Disorders Associated with Streptococcal Infection (PANDAS) Etiology for Tics and Obsessive-Compulsive Symptoms: Hypothesis or Entity? Practical Considerations for the Clinician." *Pediatrics* 113, no. 4 (2004): 883–86.

Mattsson, A., and I. Weisberg. "Behavioral Reactions to Minor Illness in Preschool Children." *Pediatrics* 46 (1970): 604–10.

Monasterio, E., R. T. Mulder, and T. D. Marshall. "Obsessive-Compulsive Disorder in Post-Streptococcal Infection." *Australian and New Zealand Journal of Psychiatry* 32 (1998): 579–81.

Moore, H. W. "Can Anorexia Nervosa Be Triggered by an Infection?" *NeuroPsychiatry Reviews* 5, no. 9 (December 2004); www.neuropsychiatryreviews.com.

Murphy, M. L., J. R. Casey, and M. E. Pichichero. "PANDAS in Primary Care Practice: Presenting Complaints, Clinical and

Lab Findings of 25 Patients with New Onset PANDAS." Abstract. *Pediatric Research* 51 (2002): 277A.

Murphy, M. L., and M. E. Pichichero. "Prospective Identification and Treatment of Children with Pediatric Autoimmune Neuropsychiatric Disorder Associated with Group A Streptococcal Infection (PANDAS)." *Archives of Pediatric and Adolescent Medicine* 156 (2002): 356–61.

Murphy, T. K., L. Snider, P. J. Mutch, E. Harden, A. Zaytoun, P. Edge, E. Storch, M. C. K. Yang, G. Mann, W. Goodman, and S. E. Swedo. "Relationships of Movements and Behaviors to Group A Streptococcus Infections in Elementary School Children." *Biological Psychiatry* 61 (2007) 279–84.

Murphy, T. K., M. Sajid, O. Soto, N. Shapira, P. Edge, M. Yang, M. Lewis, and W. Goodman. "Detecting Pediatric Autoimmune Neuropsychiatric Disorders Associated with Streptococcus in Children with Obsessive-Compulsive Disorder and Tics." *Biological Psychiatry* 55 (2004): 61–68.

Neimark, J. "Can the Flu Bring on Psychosis?" *Discover* 26, no.10 (October 2005).

Penzel, F. *The Hair Pulling Problem: A Complete Guide to Trichotillomania*. (New York: Oxford University Press, 2003): 257–60.

Perlmutter, S. J., M. A. Garvey, X. Castellanos et al. "A Case of Pediatric Autoimmune Neuropsychiatric Disorders Associated with Streptococcal Infections." *American Journal of Psychiatry* 155 (1998): 1592–98.

Perlmutter, S. J., S. F. Leitman, M. A. Garvey et al. "Therapeutic Plasma Exchange and Intravenous Immunoglobulin for Obsessive-Compulsive Disorder and Tic Disorders in Childhood." *Lancet* 354 (1999): 1153–58.

Perrin, E. M., M. L. Murphy, J. R. Casey, M. E. Pichichero, D. K. Runyan, W. C. Miller, L. A. Snider, and S. E. Swedo. "Does Group A [beta]-Hemolytic Streptococcal Infection Increase Risk for Behavioral and Neuropsychiatric Symptoms in Children?" *Archives of Pediatric and Adolescent Medicine* 158, no. 9 (2004): 848–56.

Peterson, B. S., J. F. Leckman, D. Tucker et al. "Preliminary Findings of Antistreptococcal Antibody Titers and Basal Ganglia Volumes in Tic, Obsessive-Compulsive, and Attention Deficit/Hyperactivity Disorders." *Archives of General Psychiatry* 57 (2000): 364–72.

Rapoport, J. L., G. Inoff-Germain, M. M. Weissman et al. "Childhood Obsessive-Compulsive Disorder in the NIMH MECA Study: Parent Versus Child Identification of Cases; Methods for the Epidemiology of Child and Adolescent Mental Disorders." *Journal of Anxiety Disorders* 14 (2000): 535–48.

Scahill, L., M. A. Riddle, M. McSwiggin-Hardin et al. "Children's Yale-Brown Obsessive Compulsive Scale: Reliability and Validity." *Journal of the American Academy of Child and Adolescent Psychiatry* 36 (1997): 844–52.

Shrand, H. "Behavior Changes in Sick Children Nursed at Home." *Pediatrics* 36 (1965): 604–07.

Shulman, S. T. "Pediatric Autoimmune Neuropsychiatric Disorders Associated with Streptococci (PANDAS)." *Pediatric Infectious Disease Journal* 18 (1999): 281–82.

Silva, R. R., D. M. Munoz, J. Barickman, and A. J. Friedhoff. "Environmental Factors and Related Fluctuation of Symptoms in Children and Adolescents with Tourette's Disorder." *Journal of Child Psychology and Psychiatry* 36 (1995): 305–12.

Singer, H., C. Gause, C. Morris, P. Lopez, and the Tourette Syndrome Study Group. "Serial Immune Markers Do Not Correlate with Clinical Exacerbations in Pediatric Autoimmune Neuropsychiatric Disorders Associated with Streptococcal Infections." *Pediatrics* 121 (2008): 1198–1205.

Singer, H. S. "PANDAS and Immunomodulatory Therapy." *Lancet* 354 (1999): 1137–38.

Snider, L. A., L. Lougee, M. Slattery, P. Grant, and S. E. Swedo. "Antibiotic Prophylaxis with Azithromycin or Penicillin for Childhood-Onset Neuropsychiatric Disorders." *Biological Psychiatry* 57 (2005): 788–92.

Snider, L. A., L. D. Seligman, B. R. Ketchen et al. "Tics and Problem Behaviors in Schoolchildren: Prevalence, Characterization, and Associations." *Pediatrics* 110 (2002): 331–36.

Storch, E., T. Murphy, G. Geffken, G. Mann, J. Adkins, L. Merlo, D. Duke, M. Munson, Z. Swaine, and W. Goodman. "Cognitive-Behavioral Therapy for PANDAS-Related OCD." *Journal of the American Academy of Child and Adolescent Psychiatry* 45 (2006): 1171–78.

Swedo, S. E., H. L. Leonard, M. Garvey et al. "Pediatric Autoimmune Neuropsychiatric Disorders Associated with Streptococcal Infections: Clinical Description of the First 50 Cases." *Amerian Journal of Psychiatry* 155 (1998): 264–71. (Erratum appears in *American Journal of Psychiatry* 155 [1998]: 578.)

Swedo, S. E., H. L. Leonard, and J. Rapoport. "The Pediatric Autoimmune Neuropsychiatric Disorders Associated with Streptococcal Infection (PANDAS) Subgroups: Separating Fact from Fiction." *Pediatrics* 113, no. 4 (2004): 907–11.

Swedo, S. E., L. Snider, V. Sachdev, J. MacKaronis, and M. St. Peter. "Echocardiographic Findings in the PANDAS Subgroup." *Pediatrics* 114 (2004): 748–51; originally published online on November 15, 2004.

Taranta, A. "Relation of Isolated Recurrences of Sydenham's Chorea to Preceding Streptococcal Infections." *New England Journal of Medicine* (1959): 1204–10.

Taranta, A., and G. H. Stollerman. "The Relationship of Syndenham's Chorea to Infection with Group A Streptococci." *American Journal of Medicine* 20 (1956): 170–75.

Veasy, L. G., L. Y. Tani, and H. R. Hill. "Persistence of Acute Rheumatic Fever in the Intermountain Area of the United States." *Journal of Pediatrics* 124 (1994): 9–16.

Wenner, M. "Infected with Insanity." *Scientific American Mind* 19, no. 2 (April-May 2008).

ACKNOWLEDGMENTS

MY CHILDREN ARE the people who have most shaped me. My parents—who made all things possible—my friends, and other family members are my heart. Without them, I do not know what would have become of us.

I can never say thank you enough to Sammy's doctors—Cathy Nicolaides and Dan Geller—for returning my son to me. A separate thank you to Sammy's pediatrician and psychologist for their help, to his teachers for embracing us, and to Bobbi for telling me about her son.

As with all books, this one has its own story.

I am forever grateful to Jim Sadwith. He read every draft and patiently encouraged me to find the gem buried beneath the hundreds of pages of rewrites. Sharon Bialy, proving the truism about six degrees of separation, passed the manuscript along to her college friend Anne Marie Gillen in Los Angeles. She sent it to Tristram Coburn, a literary agent who lives—as luck would have it—on the coast of Maine. He agreed to represent me and expertly landed the manuscript on the desk of my brilliant editor, Heather Jackson. Heather accepted what I thought was my very best work, encouraged me to dig deeper, and offered the polish to make it gleam. Her fingerprints are on every page.

I am deeply grateful to each of them.

Along the way, I met the intuitive Sarah M. Winslow, who insisted I was a creative artist and not only a lawyer. With author John B. Robinson, I had the most expensive lunch of my life because I bought an iBook that very afternoon (so that I could write everywhere, even in courthouse lobbies). Dr. Paul

Grant became my valued contact at the NIMH. And when I hit a dry patch, in retelling the story to photographer Lori Oransky during a leisurely island walk, I realized I had to get back to writing.

In the end, my book experience resembles successfully raising children. It took a village, an extraordinary amount of commitment, and help from the hand of a power greater than all of us.